Family Bible Study

THE Herschel HOBBS COMMENTARY

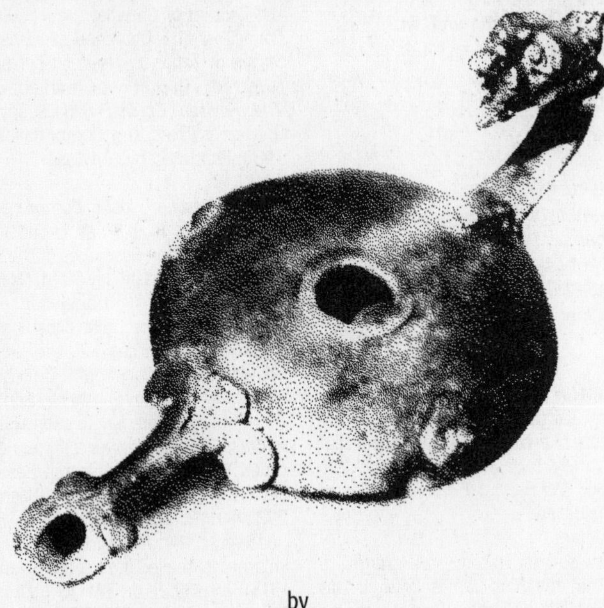

by

Robert J. Dean

SPRING 2003
Volume 3, Number 3

Send questions/comments to
Editor, *Herschel Hobbs Commentary*
One LifeWay Plaza
Nashville, TN 37234-0175
Or make comments on the web at
www.lifeway.com

ACKNOWLEDGMENTS.–We believe the Bible has God for its author; salvation for its end; and truth, without any mixture of error, for its matter and that all Scripture is totally true and trustworthy. The 2000 statement of *The Baptist Faith and Message* is our doctrinal guideline.

The Herschel Hobbs Commentary (ISSN 0191-4219), *Family Bible Study,* is published quarterly by LifeWay Christian Resources of the Southern Baptist Convention, One LifeWay Plaza, Nashville, Tennessee 37234; James T. Draper, Jr., President, and Ted Warren, Executive Vice-President, LifeWay Christian Resources of the Southern Baptist Convention; © Copyright 2002 LifeWay Christian Resources of the Southern Baptist Convention. All rights reserved. Single subscription to individual address, $20.95 per year. If you need help with an order, WRITE LifeWay Church Resources Customer Service, One LifeWay Plaza, Nashville, Tennessee 37234-0113; For subscriptions, FAX (615) 251-5818 or EMAIL subscribe@lifeway.com. For bulk shipments mailed quarterly to one address, FAX (615) 251-5933 or EMAIL CustomerService@lifeway.com. Order ONLINE at www.lifeway.com. Mail address changes to: *The Herschel Hobbs Commentary, Family Bible Study,* One LifeWay Plaza, Nashville, TN 37234-0113.

Printed in the United States of America.

Dedicated to the memory of

Fes Robertson

who used the gift of a marvelous singing voice

to glorify God and to stir and warm the hearts of others.

Contents

Study Theme

Prayer: Approaching the Throne of Grace 6

Study Theme

Who Are You, Jesus? 57

Contents

Study Theme

Study Theme

Prayer: Approaching the Throne of Grace

The Bible has many prayer promises and records many actual prayers. Among the more familiar promises is Hebrews 4:16, "Let us therefore come boldly unto the throne of grace, that we may obtain mercy, and find grace to help in time of need."

Among the lesser-known prayers of the Bible is the prayer of Jabez in 1 Chronicles 4:10. The structure of this study comes from that prayer. The prayer itself is studied only in the first lesson, but the themes of all the sessions are based on these verses.

The first lesson is "Praying That Pleases God," which relates to Jabez's prayer, "Oh that thou wouldest bless me indeed." This lesson is based on the prayer of Jabez, the prayer of Solomon for an understanding heart in 1 Kings 3, and on Ecclesiastes 5:1-7. The second lesson is "Praying About God's Kingdom," which relates to Jabez's prayer to "enlarge my coast." This lesson is based on Paul's words to the Philippians about how God gave the apostle an opportunity to witness, even when he was under arrest. The third lesson is "Praying That Focuses on God," which relates to Jabez's words "that thine hand might be with me." This third lesson is based on Daniel's prayer in Daniel 9. The fourth lesson is "Praying for Protection," which relates to Jabez's words, "that thou wouldest keep me from evil, that it may not grieve me." This lesson is based on Psalm 91. The fifth lesson, "Praying with Humility," relates to the words after Jabez's prayer, "and God granted him that which he requested." This final lesson is based on God's answer to Solomon's prayer in 2 Chronicles 7:11-22.

This study theme is designed to help you

- pray prayers that are pleasing to God (Mar. 2)
- find your place in advancing God's kingdom (Mar. 9)
- focus your prayers on God (Mar. 16)
- rely on God for protection in threatening situations (Mar. 23)
- experience God's blessings by humbly turning from sin and seeking Him (Mar. 30)

Week of March 2

PRAYING THAT PLEASES GOD

Background Passage: 1 Chronicles 4:9-10; 1 Kings 3:5-15; Ecclesiastes 5:1-7

Focal Passage: 1 Chronicles 4:9-10; 1 Kings 3:5,7-10; Ecclesiastes 5:1-7

Key Verses: 1 Chronicles 4:9-10

❖ *Significance of the Lesson*

• The *Lesson Theme* is that prayer from a pure heart pleases God. God delights in blessing those who pray with godly motives.

• The *Life Question* this lesson seeks to address is, What should I pray for?

• The *Biblical Truth* is that God has revealed in His Word the type of praying that pleases Him.

• The *Life Impact* is to help you pray prayers that are pleasing to God.

Views About Prayer

The prevailing secular mind-set either does not believe in prayer at all or may seek to use prayer for material gain or for other selfish reasons. The way many people use prayer is something akin to magic or to rubbing Aladdin's lamp. For others, prayer is little more than possessing a positive attitude or thinking good thoughts.

In the biblical worldview prayer is talking to the sovereign God, who encourages, hears, and answers the prayers of His people. The prayers of the Bible provide models of the kinds of prayers that believers of all generations are to offer to God.

Word Study: *bless*

The Hebrew word *barak* has the basic meaning "kneel" or "bow the knee" (Ps. 95:6). However, the word came to be used more often in the Old Testament to mean "bless." This word and the related word for "blessing" *(barakah)* are found repeatedly in the Old Testament. The most basic use is for people to bless God (Ps. 103:1-2). This means to praise God. The word is also used of God's blessing people (Gen. 12: 2-3). When God blesses someone, He gives His favor and does that person good. *Barak* is also used of people blessing other people, usually by praying God's blessing on them (Num. 6:24). The word is also occasionally used in asking for God's blessing for oneself (1 Chron. 4:10).

❖ *Search the Scriptures*

The prayers of Jabez and Solomon pleased God. Ecclesiastes 5:1-7 shows that prayer honors God. The three Focal Passage Outline points are designed to help you pray prayers that are pleasing to God.

Experience God's Blessing (1 Chron. 4:9-10)

Who was Jabez and why was his prayer important? What requests did he make in his prayer? Under what conditions is it right to pray for God to bless you?

1 Chronicles 4:9-10: **And Jabez was more honorable than his brethren: and his mother called his name Jabez, saying, Because I bare him with sorrow. 10And Jabez called on the God of Israel, saying, Oh that thou wouldest bless me indeed, and enlarge my coast, and that thine hand might be with me, and that thou wouldest keep me from evil, that it may not grieve me. And God granted him that which he requested.**

The early chapters of 1 Chronicles consist primarily of lists of names of people—from Adam to the end of the exile. This may seem an unlikely biblical area to provide any helpful lessons for today. Many people skim through or skip over these chapters. But almost hidden amid all the names is a short prayer of an otherwise unknown man named **Jabez.**

Jabez was an Israelite of the tribe of Judah (1 Chron. 4:1). His name means "pain." **His mother** gave him this **name** because she said, "I gave birth to him in pain" (NIV). The writer of Chronicles reported that **Jabez was more honorable than his brethren. Honorable** is a translation of the Hebrew word *kabed,* which has the basic meaning "heavy" or "weighty." In God's eyes Jabez was no spiritual lightweight but a person strong in the faith.

Jabez began his prayer to **the God of Israel** with these words: **Oh that thou wouldest bless me indeed.** In many ways this is the keynote of the prayer. Notice that Jabez did not spell out how he wanted God to bless him. He left that in God's hands. "This kind of radical trust in God's good intentions toward us has nothing in common with the popular gospel that you should ask God for a Cadillac, a six-figure income, or some other material sign that you have found a way to cash in on your connection with Him. Instead, the Jabez blessing focuses like a laser on our wanting for ourselves nothing more and nothing less than what God wants for us."[1]

In essence, Jabez's prayer was one of surrender to all that God wanted to do for him, in him, and through him. God has many blessings that He wants to give to us, but we often miss the blessings God has for us because we do not ask Him for them; and when we do ask, we make selfish requests designed only to enrich ourselves (Jas. 4:1-3).

What is the context out of which believers pray for God to bless us? For one thing, we do not ask because we deserve His blessings. His blessings are gifts of divine grace. As Jacob said in a moment of self-awareness, "I am not worthy of the least of all the mercies, and of all the truth, which thou hast showed unto thy servant" (Gen. 32:10). We come in a spirit of humility and gratitude to God for blessings.

Second, prayers for personal blessings include a commitment to be a channel of blessings to others. When God blessed Abram, He told Abram that he would be a blessing (12:1-3). The psalmist said, "God, be merciful unto us, and bless us; and cause his face to shine upon us; that thy way may be known upon earth, thy saving health among all nations" (Ps. 67:1-2).

Third, God has abundant blessings that come only when our lives are faithful and obedient to Him. For example, God promised to open the windows of heaven and pour out blessings on those who tithe (Mal. 3:10).

Fourth, we pray the same blessings for other people of faith. Numbers 6:24-26 is a beautiful benediction that shows the contents of what true blessings are and enlarges the scope to include not only "me" but "us": "The LORD bless thee and keep thee: the LORD make his face shine upon thee, and be gracious unto thee: the LORD lift up his countenance upon thee, and give thee peace." God's blessings include security, favor, grace, presence, and peace.

The second part of the prayer is **enlarge my coast** ("territory," NIV; "border," NRSV). On the surface this seems to only ask for more land. However, "from the context and results of Jabez's prayer, we can see that there was more to his request than a simple desire for more real estate. He wanted more influence, more responsibility, and more opportunity *to make a mark for the God of Israel.*"[2] The reward for the faithfulness of God's servants includes more responsibilities (see Matt. 25:21,23). Paul is a good example of this petition. He wrote to the Romans that he did not want to build on foundations laid by other missionaries, but his prayer was to take the gospel to where it had not been preached (Rom. 15:18-21).

That thine hand might be with me ("let your hand be with me," NIV) was Jabez's third request. This is a prayer of dependence on God and confidence in Him. Like all people of mature faith, Jabez had learned that he could do nothing of significance without the help and hand of the Lord. God's hand strengthens us and guides us. The basis of our assurance is not that we will never slacken our hold on the hand of the Lord, but our confidence is that His hand will hold us through all the storms of life. As Asaph wrote, "Yet I am always with you; You hold me by your right hand. You guide me with your counsel, And afterward you will take me into glory" (Ps. 73:23-24, NIV).

The fourth part of the prayer addressed to God is **that thou wouldst keep me from evil, that it may not grieve me** ("keep me from harm so that I will be free from pain," NIV; "keep me from evil, that I may not cause pain," NKJV). **Evil** translates *ra'a,* which can mean "evil" or "trouble." **Grieve** translates *'otseb,* which can mean "pain," "suffering," or "grief." This was not a request to be spared from life's griefs or pains. It was a prayer for God to keep Jabez from committing evil or from coming into situations in which he might not pass the test. A good parallel are Jesus' words in the Model Prayer: "Lead us not into temptation, but deliver us from evil" (Matt. 6:13).

The words **and God granted him that which he requested** show that Jabez's prayer pleased God. Thus it can be a model for the prayers of people of faith. Of course, the Model Prayer of Jesus is our primary model, but prayers of other believers can also instruct and inspire us to prayer what is pleasing to God.

What are the lasting lessons of 1 Chronicles 4:9-10?

1. Believers should pray for the blessings God wants to bestow on them.

2. They should pray for larger opportunities of service.

3. They should depend on the hand of God to strengthen and guide them.

4. They should ask God to deliver them from evil.

Act with Discernment (1 Kings 3:5,7-10)

Why is it a challenge to a new leader who follows a popular leader? Why did God ask Solomon what he wanted from God? What did Solomon ask for, and why did he make these requests? Why was God pleased with Solomon's prayer?

1 Kings 3:5,7-10: **In Gibeon the LORD appeared to Solomon in a dream by night: and God said, Ask what I shall give thee.**

. . . .

7 And now, O LORD my God, thou hast made thy servant king instead of David my father: and I am but a little child: I know not how to go out or come in. 8 And thy servant is in the midst of thy people which thou hast chosen, a great people, that cannot be numbered nor counted for multitude. 9 Give therefore thy servant an understanding heart to judge thy people, that I may discern between good and bad: for who is able to judge this thy so great a people? 10 And the speech pleased the Lord, that Solomon had asked this thing.

What do we know about Solomon before this incident? David had many sons by different wives. Solomon was the second son born to David and Bathsheba (2 Sam. 12:14-24). The first son died. Although Solomon was not the oldest son of David, the king promised Bathsheba that her son would be king after him. When David was old and on his deathbed, Adonijah [ad-oh-NIGH-juh], an older brother, publicly announced that he was David's successor. He was supported by some of David's former officials, including Joab, David's general. Bathsheba and Nathan went to David and told him of this. The old king then made clear to all that he named Solomon to succeed him. In the ensuing events, Adonijah and Joab were killed. All of this intrigue is recorded in 1 Kings 1–2.

The events of 1 Kings 3 took place early in Solomon's reign. Solomon loved the Lord and set out to serve Him. **Gibeon** was one of the high places at which the people worshiped. These places were forbidden after Solomon built the temple, but God accepted Solomon's worship at Gibeon as sincere. God sometimes spoke to people of faith through dreams—**the Lord appeared to Solomon in a dream by night.** Then **God said, Ask what I shall give thee** ("ask for whatever you want me to give you," NIV).

Since verse 10 says that the prayer **pleased the Lord,** we can study it as an example of a prayer that pleases God. What were the parts of Solomon's prayer? Solomon began by acknowledging the hand of God in the life of David and in his own position as king: **O Lord my God, thou hast made thy servant king instead of David my father.** Solomon recognized that he was king not because of what he had done but by God's grace.

Solomon faced the kind of challenge that confronts any new leader who follows a popular leader. In our nation's history, Harry Truman faced such a challenge when Franklin Roosevelt died suddenly. FDR had been elected president four times. The nation was in the throes of World War II. Truman felt overwhelmed suddenly to have this new responsibility. In the Bible, Joshua faced this challenge when he assumed leadership after the death of Moses. Solomon felt the same kind of uncertainty as he succeeded David. David had been king for 40 years, and he was honored as a great man and a good king. Those were big shoes for anyone to fill. Solomon felt grateful for being named king, but he felt unworthy and unprepared to fill the role. Although he was a young adult, he felt like **a little child** in the face of this task. Solomon was not looking for an excuse but expressing a sense of humility.

I know not how to go out or come in was a way of saying that Solomon did not know how to be a king over Israel. Again he called himself **thy servant** and said to God that he was **in the midst of thy people which thou hast chosen.** Not only were they **a great people** in number, but they also were God's chosen people. As king, Solomon would need to represent God to His people, and the task overwhelmed him.

Verse 9 is the heart of Solomon's prayer because here he asked for something in response to God's promise in verse 5. Solomon called himself **thy servant** a third time. Then he asked for **an understanding** ("discerning," NIV) **heart.** "This phrase literally means 'a listening heart' or 'an obedient heart.' In the Old Testament 'hearing' and 'obeying' come from the same word, a linguistic trait with practical implications. Only those who obey authority figures have really *heard* them.

Solomon must obey the Lord by keeping God's commands in order for his heart to be prepared to lead others. This listening to God will also enable him to listen to others."[3]

Solomon asked for this in order that he could fulfill his role as **judge** of God's **people.** This was one of the roles of Israel's kings. A listening and obedient heart would equip Solomon to **discern between good and bad.** People in sin confuse good and evil, right and wrong (Isa. 5:20). God shows His people what is right in order that they may do what is right and defend those who do right. This would enable the king to be an instrument of justice—something very important to the Lord and beneficial to the people.

The fact that Solomon had asked for this **pleased the Lord.** God knew that under similar circumstances many people would have asked for a long life, great riches, and victory over enemies (1 Kings 3:11). Thus the Lord not only gave Solomon what he asked for, but He also gave him riches and honor (v. 13).

What are the lasting lessons of 1 Kings 3:5,7-10?

1. Being the leader who comes after a popular leader is a great challenge.
2. Prayers always should be offered in a spirit of gratitude and humility.
3. Pray for a listening and obedient heart to the Lord.
4. Ask for discernment to judge between right and wrong and for the strength to do what is right and to defend those who do.
5. Pray in such a way as to please God.

Hear and Honor God (Eccl. 5:1-7)

*Why is Ecclesiastes difficult to understand? Why should we watch our step when we go to church? What is a **rash** mouth and a **hasty** heart? How do these verses define a **fool**? What sins of speech are committed in church? What is taught about vows? What **dreams** are referred to in verses 3 and 7?*

Ecclesiastes 5:1-7: **Keep thy foot when thou goest to the house of God, and be more ready to hear, than to give the sacrifice of fools: for they consider not that they do evil. ²Be not rash with thy mouth, and let not thine heart be hasty to utter anything before God: for God is in heaven, and thou upon earth: therefore let thy words be few. ³For a dream cometh through the multitude of**

business; and a fool's voice is known by multitude of words. [4]When thou vowest a vow unto God, defer not to pay it; for he hath no pleasure in fools: pay that which thou hast vowed. [5]Better is it that thou shouldest not vow, than that thou shouldest vow and not pay.

[6]Suffer not thy mouth to cause thy flesh to sin; neither say thou before the angel, that it was an error: wherefore should God be angry at thy voice, and destroy the work of thine hands? [7]For in the multitude of dreams and many words there are also divers vanities: but fear thou God.

Ecclesiastes is in a class by itself. Although it is one of the Wisdom Writings of the Old Testament, it is distinctive from the others. For one thing, the book seems more skeptical than any other book in the Bible. The author was brutally honest about himself and about what he observed about himself. Much of the book is a series of sayings on a variety of topics. Ecclesiastes 5:1-7 is the author's observations about religion, especially temple worship. This passage focuses on the kinds of worship and prayers that do not please God.

We expect the Bible to warn us to watch our step when we venture into areas where we might be tempted to do wrong, but with the words **keep thy foot** ("guard your steps," NIV, NRSV) **when thou goest to the house of God** the writer of Ecclesiastes warned us to watch our step when we go to church. What is so potentially dangerous about going to the place of worship? "The first thing to be careful about when you go to worship is your attitude. . . . Don't saunter in, saunter through, and saunter out of church. You have come into the presence of the awesome God. Would you so casually pay a visit to the President of the United States, or would you try to look and act your best?"[4]

G. Avery Lee offered this description of what the writer of Ecclesiastes observed of worship: "It is time for worship. The people have come from the market places, the streets, and their homes into the house of the Lord. The scene is not very inspiring. There is harsh criticism, open commercialism, decided laxity in worship, and preoccupation with things of the world. In such a mood the 'worshipers' are quick to make a vow or offer a hasty sacrifice that will relieve them of the obligations of worship and allow them to get on with the things they consider more important. After making their vows, however, the people are reluctant to put them into practice and fulfill their promises."[5]

The main concerns of the writer of Ecclesiastes were what and how people listened and spoke. **Be more ready to hear, than to give the**

sacrifice of fools, he said. This sounds much like James 1:19: "Be swift to hear, slow to speak." We have two ears and two eyes but only one mouth. This should tell us that we should see and listen more than we speak. The writer was not condemning the sacrificial system as such, but he was critical of those who offered sacrifices instead of offering genuine words and acts of worship and obedience. Such people seem blind to the **evil** they do.

Verse 2 warns of a **mouth** that is **rash** ("quick," NIV) and a **heart** that is **hasty.** People should realize that what they say (especially in God's house), they speak **before God.** Because the more we say the more likely we are to say something wrong, we should let our **words be few.** Like Solomon, we need to have listening hearts that hear and obey the Word of God. Sins of the tongue are common in everyday life and often are committed in the place of worship as well. Too often we draw near with our lips while our hearts are far from God (Matt. 15:8). God does not honor such hypocrisy. Sometimes we use our tongues to praise God and to curse people (Jas. 3:9-12). Churchgoing folk speak words of dissension (1 Cor. 1:10). Some speak boastful words (Luke 18:9-14). Some express boredom at worship (Mal. 1:10-13). Some are impatient to get out of church to get on with what they really live for (Amos 8:5-6). I recall a candid confession by a politician that he spent time in church planning his election campaign.

Verse 3 seems to have been a proverb. One possible meaning is that just as **business** worries disturb sleep, so does a **multitude of words** reveal **a fool's voice.**

Verses 4-6 focus on one particular sin of the tongue. The subject was making **a vow unto God. Defer not to pay it** means "do not delay in fulfilling it" (NIV). God has **no pleasure in fools: pay that which thou hast vowed. Better . . . not** to make a **vow** than to make a vow and not honor it. Some who made vows that they did not keep used the lame excuse **it was an error** ("My vow was a mistake," NIV). This behavior would bring judgment. The Bible is not discouraging commitments to the Lord. It is emphasizing that we are to fulfill these commitments when we have made them.

Verse 7 is a proverb like verse 3. The exact meaning is unclear, but here the word **dreams** does not refer to literal dreams or to revelations from God during sleep. Rather, it refers to one's aspirations, or as we say, one's "big dreams." The person who has big dreams also has an abundance of **vanities** to which he or she gives evidence of by using

many words. Instead of this, one should **fear** or reverence **God.**

What are the lasting lessons of Ecclesiastes 5:1-7?

1. Watch your step when you go to church.
2. Especially guard against speaking instead of listening.
3. When you make promises to God, be sure to keep them.

❖ *Spiritual Transformations*

Jabez's prayer is an example of a prayer that God answered, and thus it is a model for us. Jabez prayed for God to give him the blessings that God wanted him to have. The request of Solomon for a discerning heart pleased the Lord. Ecclesiastes 5:1-7 calls for people to listen to God and to others and warns against making vows that are not kept.

In these Bible passages we have seen basic components of the kind of prayers that please God.

What aspects of such praying are part of your prayer life? _______

____

What aspects of such praying do you need to develop or strengthen? _______________________________

____

Prayer of Commitment: Heavenly Father, teach me and lead me to pray in ways that please You. Amen.

[1]Bruce H. Wilkinson, *The Prayer of Jabez* [Sisters, Oregon: Multnomah Publishers, 2000], 24.

[2]Wilkinson, *The Prayer of Jabez,* 29.

[3]Paul R. House, "1,2 Kings," in *The New American Commentary,* vol. 8 [Nashville: Broadman & Holman Publishers, 1995], 110.

[4]L. D. Johnson, *Proverbs, Ecclesiastes, Song of Solomon,* in Layman's Bible Book Commentary, vol. 9 [Nashville: Broadman Press, 1982], 107.

[5]G. Avery Lee, *Preaching from Ecclesiastes* [Nashville: Broadman Press, 1958], 40-41.

Week of March 9

PRAYING ABOUT GOD'S KINGDOM

Background Passage: 1 Chronicles 4:9-10; Acts 16:6-15; Philippians 1:12-26
Focal Passage: Acts 16:6-10; Philippians 1:12-14,19-26
Key Verse: Philippians 1:19

❖ *Significance of the Lesson*

• The *Theme* of this lesson is that through prayer, God communicates His vision for the world. If we listen, God will reveal to us our place in enlarging His kingdom.

• The *Life Question* this lesson seeks to address is, How can I make a greater impact for God?

• The *Biblical Truth* is that believers who listen to and obey God can advance God's kingdom work in the world.

• The *Life Impact* is to help you find your place in advancing God's kingdom.

Thy Kingdom Come

In the secular worldview, the purpose of prayer, if practiced at all, typically is to make requests of God. Requests have to do with advancing the causes of those who pray, not with advancing God's kingdom. Many people approach God as a means of speaking to God, but they do not listen to God.

In the biblical worldview, prayer leads to action. Together, prayer and action enable us to be used by God to make a difference in the world. Prayer involves listening as well as speaking. God is at work in the world enlarging His kingdom, and He consistently chooses to use the prayers and actions of believers to achieve His goal.

"Enlarge My Coast"

"Enlarge my coast" was the second part of Jabez's prayer in 1 Chronicles 4:10. This year is the bicentennial of the Louisiana

Purchase. While Thomas Jefferson was president in 1803 the United States doubled its size by purchasing from France the area that is now occupied by the states of Louisiana, Arkansas, Oklahoma, Kansas, Missouri, Nebraska, Iowa, the Dakotas, Montana, most of Minnesota, and parts of Colorado and Wyoming. President Jefferson enlarged the territory of our nation and brought with it greater opportunities and responsibilities. As we noted in the previous lesson, Jabez was praying for more than mere real estate when he asked God to enlarge his territory. He was praying for greater opportunities to advance the work of God in the world. As today's believers, we should pray to God to enlarge our territory in the moral and spiritual realms of life. How can you and I make a greater impact for the advancement of the gospel? We can follow Paul's example in the four ways indicated in the Focal Passage Outline in this lesson.

Word Study: *Furtherance*

Paul used the word **furtherance** ("advance," NIV) in Philippians 1:12 to describe the advancement of the gospel and in verse 25 for the spiritual progress of the Philippians. *Prokope* means "progress," "advancement," or "furtherance." The word "was used in the Greek-speaking world to describe blazing a trail before an army, the philosophical progress toward wisdom, and the progress of a young minister."[1]

❖ *Search the Scriptures*

Paul visited Philippi on his second missionary shortly after responding to the vision of the man of Macedonia calling for someone to come and help them (Acts 16:9-10). His work in Philippi is recorded in Acts 16:12-40. Later, when he was under confinement in Rome, Paul wrote the Letter to the Philippians. He explained to the Philippians that his imprisonment in Rome had been used for good in enabling him to witness for Christ. He asked them to pray for him. He told them he was ready to depart and be with the Lord, but he was also willing to remain and continue to serve.

Listen and Obey (Acts 16:6-10)

How does God lead His people in advancing the gospel? Into what areas was Paul forbidden to enter at this time? What was the meaning of the vision? What is the significance of the word **we** *in verse 10?*

Acts 16:6-10: **Now when they had gone throughout Phrygia and
the region of Galatia, and were forbidden of the Holy Ghost** [Spirit]
**to preach the word in Asia, [7]after they were come to Mysia, they
assayed to go into Bithynia: but the Spirit suffered them not. [8]And
they passing by Mysia came down to Troas. [9]And a vision appeared
to Paul in the night; There stood a man of Macedonia, and prayed
him, saying, Come over into Macedonia, and help us. [10]And after
he had seen the vision, immediately we endeavored to go into
Macedonia, assuredly gathering that the Lord had called us for to
preach the gospel unto them.**

How does God lead you to find your place and do your part in advancing the gospel? Acts 16:6-10 describes two ways in which the Lord led Paul to find His place at this point.

On Paul's first missionary journey he visited Phrygia [FRIJ-ih-uh] and some cities in Galatia (13:13–14:20). After that journey was the Jerusalem Conference, which made decisions that Paul was asked to communicate to the Gentile churches. On the second missionary journey Paul's traveling companion was Silas. They went to the churches of Syria and Cilicia [sih-LISH-ih-uh] (chap. 15). They also revisited cities from the first journey. In doing so, Paul invited Timothy to join the team (16:1-5). Then they went **throughout Phrygia and the region of Galatia.** If you have a map of Paul's journeys in the back of your Bible, you can trace their general route. The exact route is unsure since the location of **Galatia** is debated.

At some point Paul wanted to head for **Asia.** This probably refers to the Roman province of which Ephesus was the chief city. We know Paul had wanted to go there for a long time. But at this time they **were forbidden of the Holy Ghost** [Spirit] **to preach the word in Asia.** Therefore, they continued on their way until they came to **Mysia** [MISS-ih-uh]. From there **they assayed** ("tried," NIV) **to go into Bithynia** [bih-THIN-ih-uh]. This was a province on the northern part of Asia Minor. **The Spirit** once again would not allow them to do this. We are not told how the Spirit showed them not to enter these areas, but He did in some unmistakable way. Thus having been stopped when they tried to go west and when they tried to go east, they continued to the north until they came to the coast, to the city of **Troas.**

The Spirit sometimes leads us by a series of closed and open doors. The Lord closed two doors and left Paul wondering where he was to go next. He had reached the seacoast. Where were they to go from there? Then **a vision appeared to Paul in the night.** He saw **a man of Macedonia.** Paul knew where the man was from because of what the man in the vision said: **Come over into Macedonia, and help us. Macedonia** was a province in the northern part of Greece, the area from which Alexander the Great had come several centuries earlier. Alexander had crossed from Europe into the continent of Asia and conquered much of it. Now a Christian missionary was being asked to cross from Asia to Europe with the good news of Jesus Christ.

Some believe the vision was of an actual person from Macedonia. But the vision probably was of no specific person. Many missionaries respond to God's call because of a vision of need. But even if the vision was not of an actual person, there were real people behind the vision; and Paul met them only when he responded positively to the call of the vision. Paul would never have met Lydia, the jailer, and others in Macedonia if he had ignored the vision of need. The same is true for those who respond to visions of need today.

Paul's response was to act **immediately.** The missionary team "got ready at once to leave for Macedonia, concluding that God had called us to preach the gospel to them" (NIV).

Whenever I study this passage, I remember the story of how David Livingstone was called to be a missionary to Africa. As a young medical student he at first believed he was called to be a missionary in China, but that field was hindered by the opium war. Livingstone's direction was changed when he heard Robert Moffat speak of the needs in Africa. This veteran missionary to South Africa told Livingstone of what he saw when he looked to the north in the morning sun. He saw the smoke of a thousand villages where no missionary had even been. Livingstone could not escape that vision of need. Therefore he went to Africa to bring God's light to that continent.

What are the lasting lessons of Acts 16:6-10?

1. God often leads us by closing some doors and opening another one.

2. God often calls believers to certain places and people by giving them a vision of the need.

3. Believers need to listen to and obey the Word of God and His directions.

4. When believers respond to a vision of need, they have opportunities to witness to real people who need their witness and ministry.

Use Every Opportunity (Phil. 1:12-14)

What did Paul want the Philippians to know about what had happened to him? How did he turn a difficult situation into an opportunity? What two results came of this? How did Paul's experience illustrate Romans 8:28?

Philippians 1:12-14: **But I would ye should understand, brethren, that the things which happened unto me have fallen out rather unto the furtherance of the gospel; [13]so that my bonds in Christ are manifest in all the palace, and in all other places; [14]and many of the brethren in the Lord, waxing confident by my bonds, are much more bold to speak the word without fear.**

One of the reasons Paul wrote the Letter to the Philippians was to be sure they knew **the things which happened unto** him. Epaphroditus [ih-paf-roh-DIGH-tuhs] had come from Philippi to be with Paul in Rome (Phil. 2:25-30). Paul sent him back to Philippi with this letter, so he could tell them some things. But Paul wanted to emphasize that these events, which appeared to thwart Paul's opportunities to advance the gospel, were actually used by God for its advancement. Paul had wanted to visit Rome for a long time. Now he was there, but he came as a prisoner, not as he had expected earlier. As a prisoner, he was confined and unable to move about freely as he had in the past; but Paul found that his earlier words in Romans 8:28 proved true of his confinement. God was able to bring good out of the evil that had happened to him. This is the reason for the addition of the word **rather** ("really," NIV; "actually," HCSB) when he mentioned **the things which happened unto me have fallen out rather unto the furtherance of the gospel.** Or as the *New English Bible* renders it: "Friends, I want you to understand that the work of the Gospel has been helped on, rather than hindered, by this business."

Paul mentioned two good results of his imprisonment in Rome. Verse 13 describes the first of these. The word translated **the palace** is *praitorio.* The word originally referred to the tent of a general in the Roman army. Then it had come to be used of the palace of the emperor or of a governor (Acts 23:35). But the word also was used to describe the "palace guard" (NIV)—the "imperial guard" (HCSB), the "praetorian guard" (NASB)—of several thousand elite troops who were directly attached to the emperor. They were hardened soldiers who could be brutal when the occasion called for it. Very likely Paul was guarded by one of these men day and night. Thus Paul was able to have opportunities to talk one on one with many of these soldiers. He did not claim that all of these men were won to Christ, but he did write that it had "become clear throughout the whole palace guard and to everyone else that" Paul was "in chains for Christ" (NIV).

The other good result was that Paul's faithful witness while he was a prisoner helped the Roman Christians to be more courageous witnesses for the Lord: "Because of my chains, most of the brothers in the Lord have been encouraged to speak the word of God more courageously and fearlessly" (NIV).

We ought not to reserve our witness for the most favorable circumstances. We must recognize and seize the opportunity in each set of circumstances. Some of the most powerful witnesses are those made when people are sick, dying, persecuted, or imprisoned. Non-Christians notice the way we respond to trouble. If we allow our troubles to overwhelm us, our actions say something we do not want to say. On the other hand, a faithful witness in hard times is positive in its effect for Christ.

What are the lasting lessons in Philippians 1:12-14?

1. God works all things together for good for those who love Him.
2. Christians have opportunities to witness for Christ in good times and in bad.
3. Faithful witnessing in hard times is used by God to win unbelievers and to encourage believers.

Enlist Others to Pray (Phil. 1:19)

*What did Paul mean by **my salvation**? What were two factors in Paul's confidence?*

Philippians 1:19: **For I know that this shall turn to my salvation through your prayer, and the supply of the Spirit of Jesus Christ.**

Three explanations have been given for the meaning of **my salvation.** One is that Paul was affirming his confidence of final salvation from sin and death. Paul was confident of this and often expressed his confidence (see 1:6; 2 Tim. 1:12). However, the context of verse 19 does not support that interpretation here.

A second view is that Paul was thinking of his "deliverance" (NIV) from imprisonment. Supporters of this view point to Philippians 1:25 and 2:24 to show that Paul seemed to expect to be released. Others, however, point to 1:20 and 2:17, which leave the issue in doubt. This may be what Paul meant by deliverance; however, there is a third possible meaning.

The third interpretation relates verse 19 to verse 20. Paul's central concern was that he might never fail to magnify Christ. He gave two reasons why he was confident in this area of faithful witnessing. One source of his confidence was **the supply of the Spirit of Jesus Christ.** His confidence was not in himself but in the Lord. Later in this letter he wrote, "I can do all things through Christ which strengtheneth me" (4:13). Paul relied on the guidance and power of the Spirit.

The other source of Paul's confidence was the prayers of people like the Philippians. "Paul expected them to pray for something much more significant than his release from prison. In another letter from prison Paul asked his readers to pray 'that utterance may be given me in opening my mouth boldly to proclaim the mystery of the gospel' (Eph. 6:19). He expected them to pray for him, and he expected God to answer their prayers."[2]

Have you ever heard a missionary speak and not ask the congregation to pray for the missionary and those to whom the missionary was sent? Missionaries know the power of prayer, and they depend on God's people to pray for them. Paul believed that God uses prayer to advance the gospel. He was many miles from Philippi, but their prayers would enable him to magnify the Lord.

In China, where mission work is officially banned and atheism is synonymous with the ruling Communist party, long-term workers are more aware than ever before of the necessity of an outpouring of prayer on behalf of the peoples of China. Rather than saying, "Well, if we can't do anything else, we can always pray," these workers who know that all victory is contingent on God's working are saying, "No matter what else you can do, prayer is foremost."

What are the lasting lessons of Philippians 1:19?

1. To make a greater impact for God, you should enlist others to pray for you.

2. Missionaries depend on the prayers of God's people.

3. Christian witnesses are guided and empowered by the Spirit of the Lord.

Keep on Serving (Phil. 1:20-26)

What does verse 20 reveal about Paul's objective in life? How did Paul express his confident hope of life after death? In what sense was he ready for either death or life? Which did he prefer? Why was he willing to stay?

Philippians 1:20-26: **According to my earnest expectation and my hope, that in nothing I shall be ashamed, but that with all boldness, as always, so now also Christ shall be magnified in my body, whether it be by life, or by death. 21For to me to live is Christ, and to die is gain. 22But if I live in the flesh, this is the fruit of my labor: yet what I shall choose I wot not. 23For I am in a strait betwixt two, having a desire to depart, and to be with Christ; which is far better: 24Nevertheless to abide in the flesh is more needful for you. 25And having this confidence, I know that I shall abide and continue with you all for your furtherance and joy of faith; 26that your rejoicing may be more abundant in Jesus Christ for me by my coming to you again.**

Verse 20 is one of my favorite verses in Philippians. This verse gives us insight into Paul's heart. It implies one thing he seemed to fear, and it shows his amazing commitment. His **earnest expectation and . . . hope** was that he never would **be ashamed.** This may refer to being ashamed of Christ or of being ashamed before the Lord for failing Him in some way. Stated positively, Paul wrote of his goal: **that with all boldness, as always, so now also Christ shall be magnified in my body, whether it be by life, or by death.** His objective was to exalt Jesus Christ, regardless of his own circumstances.

"What an amazing statement! Paul was not fearful or anxious about those things that concern most people; his consuming concern was one that most people give little or no attention to. The fears and anxieties of humanity are legion. People fret about money, possessions, success, prestige; they fear poverty, sickness, failure, pain, death. Paul fretted about none of these goals, nor did he fear any of these terrors. His overriding concern was to be a faithful and bold witness for Christ no matter what the circumstances. What anxiety he had about the hard realities of living and dying were focused on one goal—that he be able to honor Christ, whatever his circumstances."[3]

Paul did not expect ever to fail to magnify the Lord, but his confidence was in the Spirit and in prayers for him (v. 19). Verse 20 seems to me to be what we should seek for ourselves and what we should pray for others. It is a prayer for the best and for the worst of times. When a Christian is terminally ill, this is an appropriate prayer.

Verse 21 is an equally succinct and memorable statement of the Christian view of life and death: **For to me to live is Christ, and to die is gain.** The consuming passion of a person's life is the essential feature in what the person becomes. Paul's life was centered in Christ. He viewed all things from this perspective. Consider how other people would finish the statement "for to me to live is . . . " They might say, "making a living," "being successful," "having a good time," and so on.

It was precisely because Paul could say **for to me to live is Christ** that he could add **and to die is gain.** Paul welcomed both. Running through verses 22-26 is this twofold theme—Paul had confident hope of life after death, and he felt that he could serve Christ by continuing to live.

Notice the various ways in which Paul described his confident hope for life after death. He wrote that he had **a desire to depart, and to be with Christ.** He wrote of death as a departure from this life and an entry into a close fellowship with the Lord. The word **depart** pictures death for a believer like a ship loosing its moorings and sailing away beyond the horizon. For a while it remains visible to those on shore, but soon it disappears. When someone dies, we say, "he's gone," but someone beyond death is saying, "he's come." What is it like beyond that horizon? Paul did not satisfy our curiosity about what it will be like. He simply said we will **be with Christ.** Nothing else needs to be said.

Most of verses 22-26 deals with Paul's consideration of the two options of life or death. First he said, **I am in a strait betwixt two** ("I am torn between the two," NIV; "I am hard-pressed from both directions," NASB). Personally he preferred to go to be with the Lord, but he left this issue in God's hands. If God wanted him to continue to **live in the flesh,** Paul knew that this would be "fruitful labor" (NIV). At the time Paul wrote this letter, God seemed to be telling him that he still had work to do. Paul told the Philippians that **to abide in the flesh is more needful for you.** By continuing to live and serve, he could contribute to their **furtherance** ("progress," NIV) **and joy of faith. Furtherance** is the same word in verse 12. Paul's imprisonment had resulted in the advancement of the gospel. He felt that his release and continued service would result in the progress of the spiritual lives of the Philippians and others. Paul told the Philippians that the end result of his continuing to live would be **that your rejoicing may be more abundant in Jesus Christ for me by my coming to you again.**

F. B. Meyer contrasted Paul's words with Hamlet's words in his famous soliloquy, "To be, or not to be, that is the question." Hamlet, as Paul, weighed the issues of life and death. Life had become so unbearable that Hamlet seriously considered suicide. Yet the uncertainties and terrors of death made this option even more undesirable than continuing to face the harsh realities of his life. There are similarities between Paul and Hamlet, but there are differences also. Both weighed life and death, and both chose life. But Hamlet considered both options undesirable, and Paul considered both options desirable. Hamlet hated life, but feared death more than he hated life. Paul preferred death but welcomed continued life.[4]

Ready to go, ready to stay,
Ready my place to fill;
Ready for service, lowly or great,
Ready to do His will.[5]

When Elijah got so discouraged that he asked to die, God told him that He had things for Elijah to do before he left this world (1 Kings 19). Some of Elijah's most important work was done after this experience. Paul felt that the Lord still had work for him to do. He continued to do the Lord's work as long as the Lord gave him life. Of course, no one—not even Paul—is indispensable to the work of the kingdom. When Paul knew that his end was near, he expressed his certainty about two things: For one thing, he knew that he was going to be with the Lord. For another thing, he believed that the Lord would continue His work beyond Paul's death.

What are the lasting lessons of Philippians 1:20-26?

1. Our objective should be to magnify Christ in living and in dying.
2. Christ is the center of our living and of our dying.
3. Christians at death depart to be with the Lord.
4. We should leave in God's hands the issues of our life and death.

❖ *Spiritual Transformations*

Paul was able to make an impact in the advancement of the gospel because he listened to God and obeyed God's will. He also saw in each set of circumstances an opportunity to advance the kingdom. He relied on the Spirit of Christ and the prayers of others. He kept on serving for as long as the Lord gave him life.

Each believer can advance the gospel by following the example of Paul in the four ways outlined in this lesson. Looking at the four headings, consider what you can do to do your part.

In which of these four areas do you most need to improve? ____
____

What steps will you take to improve in that area? __________
____

Prayer of Commitment: Lord, help me to use whatever life and health and strength and days that You give me in ways that magnify You. Amen.

[1]Richard R. Melick, Jr., "Philippians, Colossians, Philemon," in *The New American Commentary*, vol. 32 [Nashville: Broadman Press, 1991], 70.

[2]Robert J. Dean, *Philippians—Life at Its Best* [Nashville: Broadman Press, 1980], 35.

[3]Dean, *Philippians*, 35.

[4]F. B. Meyer, *The Epistle to the Philippians* [London: Marshall, Morgan and Scott, 1952], 39-40.

[5]"Ready," *Baptist Hymnal* [Nashville: Convention Press,1975], No. 439.

Week of March 16

PRAYING THAT FOCUSES ON GOD

Background Passage: 1 Chronicles 4:9-10; Daniel 9:1-19
Focal Passage: Daniel 9:1-10,15-19
Key Verse: Daniel 9:18

❖ *Significance of the Lesson*

- The *Theme* of this lesson is that God's power and presence are part of His character. As we agree with God in prayer, we recognize His power and presence in the world.
- The *Life Question* this lesson seeks to address is, What kind of God do we pray to?
- The *Biblical Truth* is that God's character is the basis of prayer.
- The *Life Impact* is to help you focus your prayers on God.

To Whom Do We Pray?

In other worldviews, people either do not pray or they pray to something other than the God of the Bible. Some believe prayer does not need to be offered to any specific god; other religions pray to their own gods. Some who claim to pray to the God of the Bible have distorted views of God. Some think that prayer is just meditating with ourselves.

The biblical worldview affirms that believers can approach God in prayer not because of their goodness but because of God's character as He has revealed Himself to us. For this reason this lesson relates to the third part of Jabez's prayer, "that thine hand might be with me" (1 Chron. 4:10).

Daniel

Daniel is one of the most extraordinary people of the Bible. He was a man of strong convictions who boldly stood for those convictions. As a young man and an exile in a foreign land, he refused to eat the meat and drink the wine from the king's table. Daniel was able to serve God faithfully in a pagan land and even rise to high government office in that land. He was a man of prayer whose commitment to his prayer routine resulted in his being thrown into the den of lions, from which God delivered him. He was given the gift of interpreting dreams, signs, and visions. He was taken to Babylon as a young man in 605 B.C. and was still living in 535 B.C. He served in two of the ancient world's great empires—Babylon and Persia.

Word Study: *incline thine ear*

In Daniel 9:18 Daniel beseeched God to "incline thine ear." The Hebrew word *nata* means "stretch out," "spread out," "extend," "incline," or "bend." The word is often used with "ear." This phrase was sometimes used of pupils being challenged to pay attention (Prov. 22:17) and of people needing to listen to God (Jer. 7:24). It is also used in prayers beseeching God to hear and answer prayers (2 Kings 19:16).

❖ *Search the Scriptures*

Daniel prayed an earnest prayer of confession of sins to God on behalf of Israel. Inspired by Jeremiah's prophecy of the return from exile after 70 years, he prayed to the great God of all things. He contrasted the people's sins with the righteousness of God. He concluded with a plea for God to show mercy and to fulfill His promise.

What kind of God do we pray to? The three outline points help to answer that question.

God Is Great (Dan. 9:1-4)

What aspects of God's greatness are seen in the following words: ***which was made . . . the word of the Lord . . . prayer . . . my God . . . the great and dreadful God****?*

Verses 1-2: **In the first year of Darius the son of Ahasuerus, of the seed of the Medes, which was made king over the realm of the Chaldeans; 2In the first year of his reign I Daniel understood by books the number of the years, whereof the word of the Lord came to Jeremiah the prophet, that he would accomplish seventy years in the desolations of Jerusalem.**

Since Daniel was a young man in 605 B.C., he was an old man in Daniel 9 **in the first year of Darius,** which was 538 B.C. But he was still a vigorous man of faith. His discipline of praying three times a day was so sure that his enemies used his faithfulness to accuse him before the king (Dan. 6).

God's greatness is seen in several ways in verses 1-4. First it is seen in the way He moved in the affairs of nations to bring in His kingdom. This is implied by the words **which was made.** These words show that **Darius** did not come to the throne by chance but by divine appointment. God's sovereign rule and active involvement in history is seen in Daniel's interpretation of Nebuchadnezzar's dream of the image made of various substances (Dan. 2). This idea of the providence of God in human history is found throughout the Bible.

Books translates *separim.* The literal meaning is "writings." It could be rendered "rolls" or "scrolls." The *New International Version* translates it as "Scriptures." Daniel referred to **the word of the LORD** that **came to Jeremiah the prophet.** Daniel was thinking specifically of God's promise **that he would accomplish seventy years in the desolations of Jerusalem.** Daniel probably had been reading Jeremiah 25:11-12, which promises the defeat of the Babylonians after 70 years, and Jeremiah 29:10, which promised the exiles in Babylon that God would deliver them after 70 years. Daniel understood these words of the scroll to be the word of God to His people.

Thus a second way God's greatness is seen in these verses is in the written Word of God. The very existence of the Scripture reveals a great God. And the Bible itself is a testimony to God's greatness. God revealed Himself, inspired those who wrote His Word, and illumines the minds of those who read. Daniel was moved by the words of Jeremiah.

Verses 3-4: **And I set my face unto the Lord God, to seek by prayer and supplications, with fasting, and sackcloth, and ashes:**
4and I prayed unto the LORD my God, and made my confession, and said, O Lord, the great and dreadful God, keeping the covenant and mercy to them that love him, and to them that keep his commandments.

Bible study and prayer go together. When Daniel read the Word of God from the prophet Jeremiah, he was moved to pray. Verse 3 is a statement of his commitment to pray. This points to a third way in which God's greatness is seen in these verses. God hears and answers prayer. Only the great One-and-Only God actually hears and answers prayer.

Verse 3 shows the intensity of the prayer that Daniel was about to make. In verse 4 Daniel used both praying that focuses on gods for **the LORD my God** to whom he was to pray. This combination of the general and personal names for God depicts His greatness. **Supplications** are "petitions" (NIV). Daniel's prayer was done with **fasting,** showing his total concentration on the Lord. **Sackcloth** and **ashes** were used by the Jews to express deep emotion. When you stop and think about the miracle of prayer, you cannot fail to recognize that only a great God can be approached in this way and respond as He does.

The fourth way this passage points to God as great is in the first part of verse 4. God is called **the great and dreadful** ("awesome," NIV) **God.** The word for **great** is combined with a word that denotes fear and trembling—**dreadful** *(yare').* When we pray, we come into the presence of the Creator and Judge of the earth. We should come with awe and reverential fear. This great God is so great that our minds cannot fully comprehend Him: "O the depth of the riches both of the wisdom and knowledge of God! how unsearchable are his judgments, and his ways past finding out!" (Rom. 11:33). But the paradox is that although our minds cannot fathom God and His ways, we can truly know Him and trust Him. Thus Daniel called this awesome God, **my God.** Our relationship with God is not a buddy-buddy relationship, but it is personal and real. Through Jesus Christ, we are invited to come boldly to His throne of grace (Heb. 4:16).

The last part of verse 4 is the opening of Daniel's prayer. His words point to another aspect of God's greatness—His faithfulness. God made a **covenant** with the Israelites, and He had been faithful to His part of that covenant. **Mercy** is the word *hesed,* which refers to faithfulness to the covenant.

Sometimes we forget that prayer is addressed to this great God. What are the ways in which verses 1-4 reveal that God is great?

1. God is great because He moves in the affairs of nations to bring in His kingdom.

2. God is great because He revealed, inspired, and preserved His written Word.

3. God is great in hearing and answering prayer.

4. God is great in allowing us to know Him, although He is the Almighty God.

5. God is great because of His faithfulness to His covenant promises to His people.

God Is Righteous (Dan. 9:5-10,15-16)

How does the righteousness of God set Him apart from other gods? How does the righteousness of God reveal the unrighteousness of human beings? What sins of Israel did Daniel confess? How does God's righteousness show itself to be just? How does His righteousness act to bring about deliverance?

Verses 5-10: **We have sinned, and have committed iniquity, and have done wickedly, and have rebelled, even by departing from thy precepts and from thy judgments: 6Neither have we hearkened unto thy servants the prophets, which spake in thy name to our kings, our princes, and our fathers, and to all the people of the land. 7O Lord, righteousness belongeth unto thee, but unto us confusion of faces, as at this day; to the men of Judah, and to the inhabitants of Jerusalem, and unto all Israel, that are near, and that are far off, through all the countries whither thou hast driven them, because of their trespass that they have trespassed against thee. 8O Lord, to us belongeth confusion of face, to our kings, to our princes, and to our fathers, because we have sinned against thee. 9To the Lord our God belong mercies and forgivenesses, though we have rebelled against him; 10neither have we obeyed the voice of the LORD our God, to walk in his laws, which he set before us by his servants the prophets.**

The word **righteousness** is in verses 7, 16, and 18. The Hebrew word is *saddiq*. The related word "righteous" in verse 14 is *s^{e}daqa*. The basic meaning of the word is "straightness." It often refers to God as the source of true holiness, goodness, and integrity. "Righteousness to the Israelite mind was no abstract principle or characteristic of an impersonal moral order. It is a definite quality of the Divine personality, standing over all norms and laws as well as in them. God is righteous in that he reveals to men what is right and helps to achieve the right which is due a righteous people."[1]

God's righteousness is in marked contrast to the unrighteousness of pagan gods and of humanity apart from God's grace and power. Pagan gods are the creations of human minds and hands. Not surprisingly, therefore, the gods have the same faults and sins as the humans who created them. The Bible reveals a God who is righteous and who expects His people to live righteous lives. The pagan gods make no such demands on their worshipers.

Daniel's prayer is basically a confession of the sins of Israel, sins that were so serious and persistent that the Israelites were defeated and carried into exile. Verse 5 lists these sins. **Sinned** is a general word that means "to miss the mark" or "to fall short of the standard." **Iniquity** is a word that refers to something that is twisted and perverted. **Done wickedly** refers to gross sins against other human beings and against God. **Rebelled** was their basic sin. They rebelled **by departing from** God and His commandments.

We know from verse 2 that Daniel was reading Jeremiah 25:11-12. In Jeremiah 25:1-10 are listed the sins for which the Israelites were being punished. The theme of these verses is that the people had rejected God by rejecting the prophets He sent (Jer. 25:4). This is the same charge made by Daniel in verse 6. Daniel repeated the charge in verse 10. It is easier to honor dead prophets than to listen to living ones. Jesus accused the Pharisees of building the tombs of the prophets but of following the example of their ancestors, who killed the prophets (Matt. 23:29-32).

Verse 7 contrasts the **righteousness** of God and the people's shameful living. **Confusion of faces** literally means "shame of face." Some people speak of the "loss of face," by which they mean something that shames and dishonors them. This was true of people at all levels of society: **our kings . . . our princes . . . our fathers . . . all the people of the land.** It also included not only the people of **Judah** but also the people of the Northern Kingdom of **Israel,** who had been taken captive over a century earlier by the Assyrians.

Verses 8-10 reinforce the messages of verses 5-7 by repeating the key ideas. Verse 9 introduces the reality of God's **mercies and forgiveness,** for which I will save my comments until verses 17-19.

A person's prayer life, or lack of such a life, is a sign of his or her spiritual health or disease. A godless man was caught in a storm at sea. He feared that he would be killed. His shipmates urged him to join them in praying for deliverance. Finally he yielded to their plea. He prayed: "O Lord, I have not asked you for anything for fifteen years, and if you deliver us out of this storm and bring us safe to land again, I promise that I will not bother you again for another fifteen years!"[2]

Verses 15-16: **And now, O Lord our God, that hast brought thy people forth out of the land of Egypt with a mighty hand, and hast gotten thee renown, as at this day; we have sinned, we have done wickedly. [16]O Lord, according to all thy righteousness, I beseech**

thee, let thine anger and thy fury be turned away from thy city Jerusalem, thy holy mountain: because for our sins, and for the iniquities of our fathers, Jerusalem and thy people are become a reproach to all that are about us.

Verses 11-14 form the bridge from verse 10 to verse 15. These verses spell out another aspect of God's righteousness, which is implicit throughout Daniel's prayer. God's righteousness is revealed in the justice of His punishment of Israel for persistent sinning.

Verses 15-16 are Daniel's prayer that God would fulfill His promise in Jeremiah 29:10 and deliver Israel from their plight. In verse 15 Daniel recalled God's great past deliverance in Israel's history. The Bible never refers to the exodus from Egypt as an escape engineered by Moses or the people. Rather it was the **Lord our God, that hast brought thy people forth out of the land of Egypt with a mighty hand.** This divine deliverance had brought God **renown.**

Daniel prayed that the Lord would now show His righteous deliverance by bringing His people back from captivity. Daniel beseeched the Lord **according to all** the Lord's **righteousness** to turn **away** His **anger** and **fury** from **Jerusalem.** In other words, Daniel used the word **righteousness** in the sense of *deliverance.* We are familiar with this use of the righteousness of God from Paul's Letter to the Romans. The atoning death of Jesus showed God's righteousness (Rom. 3:21-26) and is our deliverance.

What are the lasting lessons of Daniel 9:5-10,15-16?

1. God is righteous and the source and standard for human righteousness.
2. God's righteousness reveals and judges human sin.
3. Sin is basically rebellion against the God of faithfulness and love.
4. God is righteous and just in condemning sinners.
5. God's righteousness reveals itself in acts of deliverance for His people.

God Is Merciful (Dan. 9:17-19)

What earlier references to God's mercy are in Daniel 9:1-16? Why can we not study any one attribute of God in isolation from His total being? What are the parts of the prayer for God to show mercy toward Israel? How does verse 18 reflect the New Testament doctrine of salvation by grace?

Verses 17-19: **Now therefore, O our God, hear the prayer of thy servant, and his supplications, and cause thy face to shine upon thy sanctuary that is desolate, for the Lord's sake.**
18O my God, incline thine ear, and hear; open thine eyes, and behold our desolations, and the city which is called by thy name: for we do not present our supplications before thee for our righteousnesses, but for thy great mercies.
19O Lord, hear; O Lord, forgive; O Lord, hearken and do; defer not, for thine own sake, O my God: for thy city and thy people are called by thy name.

The lesson outline identifies three aspects of God's being that define the God to whom we pray. In general, each of these fits the main theme of the verses to which it is referenced. However, none of these can be isolated from the others. God is great, but His greatness includes His righteousness and His mercy. God is righteous, but His righteousness is great and merciful. God is merciful, and this mercy is part of what makes Him great and of what constitutes His righteousness.

Prior to verse 17 are several references to God's mercy. The word "mercy" in verse 4 is *hesed,* which is the covenant love of God, often translated "lovingkindness" (NASB). The word "mercies" in verse 9 is *rah^{a}mim,* the same word for **mercies** in verse 18. This word is often translated "tender mercies." Both Hebrew words appear together in Psalm 103:4 in a list of blessings ("lovingkindness and tender mercies"). The word "forgivenesses" *(s^{e}liha)* in verse 9 is from the same root as **forgive** in verse 19. This word is used exclusively of God in the Old Testament, for only He can forgive sin.

Daniel's prayer is a model for prayer. He began with reverent praise for the great and awesome God. Then he confessed Israel's sins. Finally he asked God to show His mercy by forgiving His people. Thus the stages of prayer are adoration, confession, and petition and intercession.

Notice the stages in the process of forgiveness. Daniel asked God to **hear the prayer** and to **behold our desolations.** This was a way of calling for God to be moved with compassion as He looked upon the plight of His people. Daniel asked the Lord to **cause** His **face to shine upon** His **sanctuary.** This was a prayer for the Lord to show His favor for His **desolate** temple and desolate people. Daniel made plain that these earnest prayers were not based on their **righteousnesses** but on God's **great mercies.** Then Daniel asked God to **forgive** His people. In the last part of verse 19 Daniel called on God to **do** something. In light of the total prayer this referred to God's carrying out the promise of Jeremiah 29:10 and restoring the people not only to Himself but also to their native land.

One of the most striking things in verses 17-19 is the reflection of the New Testament doctrine of salvation by God's grace, not by human works or righteousness. Verse 18 spells it out: "We do not make requests of you because we are righteous, but because of your great mercy" (NIV). Compare this with Titus 3:4-5: "But when the kindness and love of God our Savior appeared, he saved us, not because of righteous things we had done, but because of his mercy" (NIV).

The most significant thing about the biblical view of prayer is the God to whom we pray. What are the lasting lessons of Daniel 9:17-19?

1. The great and righteous God of mercy is the one true God.

2. Prayer includes adoration, confession of sins, petition and intercession.

3. The most distinctive thing about Christian prayer is the God to whom we pray.

4. None of us can base our prayers on our own righteousness; we must cast ourselves on the mercy of a loving God.

❖ *Spiritual Transformations*

Daniel prayed after reading God's prophecy through Jeremiah concerning the end of Israel's captivity. He prayed to the great and awesome God, for whom all things are possible. He confessed Israel's sins against the righteous God. He asked the God of mercy to forgive and restore Israel.

This lesson deals with some crucial issues about our prayer life. Here are three:

Daniel prayed daily and more than once a day (Dan. 6:10). When and where do you pray? ____________________

How do you keep your prayers focused on God and not on yourself?

____

Do you pray to the God of the Bible or to a god of your own invention? ____________________

Prayer of Commitment: Almighty God, our Father, forgive our sins and help us pray and live by Your grace. Amen.

[1]G. Ernest Wright, *The Challenge of Israel's Faith* [Chicago: The University of Chicago Press, 1944], 58.

[2]Clarence E. Macartney, *Macartney's Illustrations* [Nashville: Abingdon Press, 1946], 268-269.

Week of March 23

PRAYING FOR PROTECTION

Background Passage: 1 Chronicles 4:9-10; Psalm 91:1-16
Focal Passage: Psalm 91:1-16
Key Verse: Psalm 91:15

❖ *Significance of the Lesson*

• The *Theme* of this lesson is that God hears and answers prayers for deliverance.

• The *Life Question* this lesson seeks to address is, How will God respond to my prayers for protection?

• The *Biblical Truth* is that God hears and is able to answer the prayers of His people when they turn to Him for protection in threatening situations.

• The *Life Impact* is to help you rely on God for protection in threatening situations.

Security

In a secular worldview, people look to earthly sources for security. They trust in wealth, success, technology, weapons, families, or themselves for security and protection from threatening situations.

In the biblical worldview, real security comes from trusting God and entrusting ourselves to Him. God is able to protect and deliver His people in threatening situations. He hears and answers His people's prayers when they turn to Him for help.

Word Study: *refuge*

The English word **refuge** in verses 2 and 9 is the noun *mahseh.* It is also found in Psalm 46:1, "God is our refuge and strength." A refuge is a place to which one goes in time of danger. It provides safety in such times.

❖ *Search the Scriptures*

God is the true source of security for those who trust in Him. Because of this, people of faith should not live in fear of the realities that threaten them. God will protect those who trust in Him. He has promised to be with those who call on Him in trouble.

The Focal Passage Outline points tell us four things God will do in response to our prayers for protection.

Strengthen My Faith (Ps. 91:1-2)

What four names for God are used in these verses? What four words describe God as a source of security? Why is true faith always personal?

Verses 1-2: **He that dwelleth in the secret place of the most High shall abide under the shadow of the Almighty. [2]I will say of the LORD, He is my refuge and my fortress: my God; in him will I trust.**

Four names for God strengthen the impression of Him as the true source of security: **the most High . . . the Almighty . . . the LORD . . . God.** Melchizedek blessed Abram in the name of "the most high God, possessor of heaven and earth" (Gen. 14:19). The Lord revealed Himself to Abram as "the Almighty God" (17:1). **God** is used in Genesis 1:1 and is the general term for God. **The LORD** is the name *Yahweh,* the personal name of God.

Four words describe God as the source of security. **Secret place** ("shelter," NIV) refers to what is covered or hidden. "For in the time of trouble he shall hide me in his pavilion: in the secret of his tabernacle shall he hide me; he shall set me up upon a rock" (Ps. 27:5). **Shadow** may reflect the custom of the time that when one dwelt in the tent of his host, the host became the guarantee of the safety of the guest. Or it may reflect the analogy of dwelling beneath the shadow of the wings of the Almighty as a baby bird is safe beneath the wings of the parent bird (see Ps. 91:4). For comments on the word **refuge,** see the "Word Study" at the beginning of this lesson. **Fortress** is a stronghold. It is more than a fort; it is a fortified position. People tend to trust in human fortresses as impregnable protection against their enemies. But there are no such human fortresses. History has taught us that lesson.

Notice the emphasis on personal faith. The word **my** is used three times: **my refuge . . . my fortress . . . my God.** Verses 1-2 end with the psalmist's personal declaration of faith: **in him will I trust.**

Think of all the words we use before the word *security.* We speak of national security, financial security, social security, home security, and so forth. Most of us realize that none of these is truly secure. In spite of our best efforts, none of them can be the basis of the kind of trust of which only God is worthy.

Under the shadow of Thy throne
Thy saints have dwelt secure;
Sufficient is Thy arm alone,
And our defense is sure.[1]

What lasting lessons are in verses 1-2?

1. God is the only source of true security.
2. We should place our trust in Him.
3. True faith is always personal.

Calm My Fears (Ps. 91:3-8)

What words describe the things people fear? Should we take these as literal or figurative? What words does God use to calm our fears? Why did the psalmist mention the fate of the wicked?

Verses 3-6: **Surely he shall deliver thee from the snare of the fowler, and from the noisome pestilence. [4]He shall cover thee with his feathers, and under his wings shalt thou trust: his truth shall be thy shield and buckler. [5]Thou shalt not be afraid for the terror by night; nor for the arrow that flieth by day; [6]nor for the pestilence that walketh in darkness; nor for the destruction that wasteth at noonday.**

Verse 3 lists two fears. **Fowler** means "trapper" (NASB). **The snare of the fowler** refers to things in life that ensnare and trap us. They are unexpected dangers that will place us in jeopardy. They are traps for the unwary. **The noisome** ("deadly," NIV, NASB) **pestilence** may be a literal plague or epidemic, or it may represent the kinds of troubles that are like a plague. Whether we take the trap and the plague as literal or figurative, they represent things that are real. They are real not in the sense that all of them come to each person, for some of our worse fears never materialize. They are real in that they do exist in our imperfect world. In either case, we should **not be afraid.**

God promises to people of faith that **he shall deliver** them from these things. Throughout this psalm, we need to ask if this means *from* all such things or *through* such things? There is a difference in saying that we will never face such things and saying that we will face some of these things but God will deliver us through them. The two analogies seem to imply deliverance *through* threatening situations. The analogy in verse 4 is that of a parent bird protecting the small birds: **He shall cover thee with his feathers, and under his wings shalt thou trust.**

The other analogy in verse 4 comes from the military: **his truth shall be thy shield and buckler.** God equips us to withstand the evil forces that threaten us.

The terror by night can refer to any of the many fears that come with the darkness. For many people **night** is a time of fear. Sometimes the dangers are real; often they are the result of numerous fears of what might happen. A Cornish prayer says:

From ghoulies and ghosties and long-leggety beasties
And things that go bump in the night, Good Lord, deliver us![2]

Terror is an appropriate word for many of the fears that people feel today. The rest of the world has lived with terrorism for years, but it is a new experience for many Americans. Some Americans have lived for many years with terror at **night** because of crime and gangs, but now all are aware of the possibility of terrorists among us seeking to do harm. These fears often come at night. Commenting on the dangers in verses 2-6, Derek Kidner wrote, "Most of these dangers are of a kind which strike unseen, against which the strong are as helpless as the weak."[3]

The arrow that flieth by day usually is not seen until it strikes; and even if it is seen, it seldom can be dodged. **The arrow** signifies any deadly force that might strike us in the course of any day.

Verse 6 is parallel to verse 5. It warns of **the pestilence that walketh** ("stalks," NIV) **in darkness** and **the destruction that wasteth at noonday. Pestilence** is mentioned again because epidemics and plagues were so common and so deadly in that day. A plague "sometimes seems to run its deadly course in the darkness of the night; then again it marches abroad boldly in the very heat of the day, perhaps even being aided by a muggy heat that prevails."[4]

The things mentioned in verses 3-6 are things that breed fear. They are threatening situations, but believers should not become paralyzed by fear of them. Rather, we should trust God. When fear knocks at the door, send faith to answer it. David wrote, "What time I am afraid, I will trust in thee" (Ps. 56:3). And the apostle Paul wrote to Timothy, "For God hath not given us the spirit of fear; but of power, and of love, and of a sound mind" (2 Tim. 1:7).

An old Arabian story tells of a traveler who met the dreadful figure of Pestilence just outside the gates of a city. He asked Pestilence how many lives he would take in the city. Pestilence said, "I will take 5,000." Actually 50,000 died. The next time the traveler saw Pestilence, he asked why Pestilence had slain 50,000 instead of 5,000. Pestilence replied, "I kept my promise. I took only 5,000 lives. It was Fear which took the rest!"[5]

Verses 7-8: **A thousand shall fall at thy side, and ten thousand at thy right hand; but it shall not come nigh thee. 8Only with thine eyes shalt thou behold and see the reward of the wicked.**

Verse 7 sounds like the testimony of a survivor of some threatening situation. Many survivors of war feel this way. They have seen others fall all around them, but somehow they are still alive. Survivors of other disasters have similar feelings. They often ask, "Why did the Lord spare me?" At such times we should be careful what conclusions we draw from survival. First of all, all such survivals are of the Lord. It is only by His grace that we live and move and have our being. Life is fragile, and it is the gift of God who gave it and sustains it. Second, we must beware of assuming that we will always be delivered. "The faith of the children of God does not necessarily anticipate that harm will never come to them. What extreme statements like this one mean is that it is possible for God to defend His own in cases of seemingly inescapable dangers, and He will frequently do so."[6] Third, do not assume that you are being delivered because you are better than those who have perished. Jesus mentioned two disasters of His day. He asked some survivors if they thought they were better than those who perished. He told them that they were not, but that disaster is always a call for each person to search his own heart and to repent (Luke 13:1-5).

The mention of **the reward** ("punishment," NIV) **of the wicked** in verse 8 is not intended as a call to gloat over the fate of the wicked or to support the view that suffering or death is always punishment for sin. Survivors are not necessarily better people than those who do not survive. Some perceptive survivors of terrible ordeals testify that the best of the people were those who perished, because they often died by giving themselves for others.

What are the lasting lessons of verses 3-8?

1. At some time everyone faces threatening situations.
2. Such fears threaten to paralyze people.
3. People of faith should not fear such situations.
4. God is able to deliver from such troubles.
5. Survivors should thank God, not feel they are better than those who do not survive.

Guard My Steps (Ps. 91:9-13)

What part of the Model Prayer is similar to verse 10? What is the difference between faith and presumption? How did Satan misuse verses 11-12? What is the meaning and application of verse 13?

Verses 9-10: **Because thou hast made the LORD, which is my refuge, even the most High, thy habitation; [10]there shall no evil befall thee, neither shall any plague come nigh thy dwelling.**

Verse 9 picks up the message of verses 1-2 and assumes that someone has such trust in the Lord. **My refuge** is in both passages as is the title **most High. Thy habitation** means "your dwelling" (NIV). Verse 10 seems to promise the kind of deliverance or exemption from **evil** implied in verse 7. **Evil** is a word that can refer to moral evil or to the troubles and calamities that sometimes befall people. Since **evil** is used in verse 10 as parallel to **plague,** the meaning here seems to be trouble. Verse 10 is another of the verses in Psalm 91 that needs to be qualified in some way by Bible teachings as a whole.

Verses 11-12: **For he shall give his angels charge over thee, to keep thee in all thy ways. [12]They shall bear thee up in their hands, lest thou dash thy foot against a stone.**

These verses are familiar to Christians because Satan quoted them during one of the temptations of Jesus. Satan had told Jesus to jump from the high point in the temple: "And saith unto him, If thou be the Son of God, cast thyself down: for it is written, he shall give his angels charge concerning thee: and in their hands they shall bear thee up, lest at any time thou dash thy foot against a stone" (Matt. 4:6). In other words, the devil quoted Psalm 91:11-12, claiming that it was a promise that God would send His angels to save Jesus from harm, even if He jumped from the temple's pinnacle. Jesus saw the flaw in this interpretation and application. He replied by quoting Deuteronomy 6:16: "Thou shalt not tempt the Lord thy God" (Matt. 4:7). This passage shows for one thing that the devil can quote Scripture when he thinks it serves his cause. It also shows that Jesus saw through this smoke screen.

Jesus knew the difference between faith and presumption. Faith trusts God and leaves the outcome in His hands. It is aggressive in moving ahead by faith, but it doesn't take unnecessary risks and then expect God to protect us.

This misuse of Psalm 91:11-12 is a warning that applies to the entire psalm. It would be easy to take many of these verses in ways that lead to presumption rather than to faith.

What then is the message of verses 11-12? God does promise the help of His angels in watching over us, protecting us, and in delivering us. He does use our believing prayers to accomplish this, but God is the One who decides when and how to deliver us.

A man recalled what his mother had told him when he was frightened. He was a child when Haley's Comet made one of its infrequent appearances to people on earth. He was asleep, but his parents knew this was a once-in-a-lifetime opportunity to see this display in the heavens. So they woke him up and brought him outside. He was terrified by the colorful and brilliant sky. He clung to his mother in fear. He never forgot what he asked her and what she said. He asked, "Mother, what will happen if it falls on us?" She replied, "Don't worry; God will take care of you." In telling this experience, he commented that he knew even then that she was not promising that God would surround them with a magic shield. He knew she meant that we can trust God no matter what happens.

***Verse 13:* Thou shalt tread upon the lion and adder: the young lion and the dragon shalt thou trample under feet.**

Faith leads to bold actions on behalf of God's kingdom. Like David, we should be willing to face the giants and other powerful enemies of the Lord and His people. However, this must be done in obedience to the Lord and armed with His strength.

The positive message of verse 13 is that when we enter the fray at God's biding and in His strength, the victory is the Lord's victory because, as the story of David and Goliath shows, "The battle is the LORD'S" (1 Sam. 17:47).

What are the lasting lessons of verses 9-13?

1. Those who trust the Lord will be delivered from evil. At times this means that we will not have to face the trouble. At other times it means that we shall be delivered through the trouble.

2. Faith is not presuming that no matter what we do the Lord will deliver us.

3. Faith is not timid but bold. God uses true faith to win victories over evil.

Answer My Prayers (Ps. 91:14-16)

What three human responses are mentioned? What eight promises did God make? When is it right to pray for protection or deliverance from threatening situations?

Verses 14-16: **Because he hath set his love upon me, therefore will I deliver him: I will set him on high, because he hath known my name. [15]He shall call upon me, and I will answer him: I will be with him in trouble; I will deliver him, and honor him. [16]With long life will I satisfy him, and show him my salvation.**

The dominant feature of these verses is the eightfold promise of the Lord to His people, but the three human responses also are important. God is the **I** and **my** in these verses, and the **he** and **him** is the believer. Therefore, when the psalmist wrote **he hath set his love upon me,** he was referring to the love that believers have for the Lord.

The second human response is **he hath known my name.** In the Bible, one's name stood for the person. Thus in knowing God's **name,** they knew the Lord. God's name is given in Exodus 34:6-7.

He shall call upon me is the third human response. This refers to one's basic faith, especially expressed in prayer to the Lord. Those who truly **call upon** the Lord do so not just in times of threatening situations. Such prayers are appropriate whenever certain conditions exist. God protects us many times when we are not aware of the danger, but He often conditions His deliverance on our prayers. It is always right to call on the Lord for help.

Notice the Lord's eight promises. The promises are: **I will deliver** ("rescue," NIV) **him . . . I will set** ("protect," NIV) **him on high . . . I will answer him . . . I will be with him in trouble . . . I will deliver him . . .** I will **honor him . . . with long life I will satisfy him . . .** I will **show him my salvation.** The repetition of **I** shows that deliverance and help in such situations comes from the Lord, not from us.

Daniel 3:16-18 is a good passage on the subject of praying for deliverance from threatening situations. The three Hebrew young men were told they would be thrown into the fiery furnace if they did not bow down to Nebuchadnezzar's image. Their reply is classic. They emphasized that they knew their God was able to deliver them and would deliver them. However, they added that even if He chose not to deliver them from this threat, they still would not disobey Him. We believe that God is always able to do whatever He chooses to do. Faith, however, includes not only confidence of His power but also trust in His love. God was able, but He might have chosen not to deliver them. Even so, they trusted God.

God does not always deliver us from danger and even death, but He delivers us through these things—even when the disaster kills us, we are still with the Lord. In Luke 21:12-18 Jesus predicted that His followers would be persecuted and even put to death. But Jesus promised, "There shall not a hair of your head perish" (v. 18). How can that be? Jesus' point is that people may kill you, but they cannot harm the real you. You have the assurance of life after death. When we encounter threatening situations, what is the worst that could happen? We could lose our lives. But for believers, this is not the end; it is the beginning.

What are the lasting lessons of verses 14-16?

1. People of faith call on the Lord at all times, including when they are in threatening situations.

2. God is able to deliver His people *from* trouble, but He often delivers them *through* troubles.

3. Since God leads us through death to life, even when we die, we are with Him.

❖ *Spiritual Transformations*

We should trust in God, who is our only ultimate source of security. Although we live in a world of fearful things, we should not be afraid. God will deliver His people. He promises to be with them in trouble and to deliver them from or through their troubles.

The testimony that I often hear is this, "I would not have made it without the help of the Lord." *How does relying on the Lord day by day help in threatening situations?* ______________________________

____

How do you handle the fears that come at such times? __________
____

For what do you pray at such times? ______________________

Prayer of Commitment: Almighty God, deliver me from those things that threaten my ability to do Your will. Amen.

[1]Isaac Watts, "O God, Our Help in Ages Past," *The Baptist Hymnal* [Nashville: Convention Press, 1991], No. 74.

[2]Cornish prayer, cited in *Bartlett's Familiar Quotations*, 15th edition revised and enlarged [Boston: Little, Brown and Company, 1980], 921.

[3]Derek Kidner, *Psalms 73–150*, in the Tyndale Old Testament Commentaries [Downers Grove: InterVarsity Press, 1975], 332.

[4]H. C. Leupold, *Exposition of the Psalms* [Grand Rapids: Baker Book House, 1969], 653.

[5]Charles Wellborn, *This Is God's Hour* [Nashville: Broadman Press, 1952], 52.

[6]Leupold, *Exposition of the Psalms*, 653.

Week of March 30

PRAYING WITH HUMILITY

Background Passage: 1 Chronicles 4:9-10; 2 Chronicles 7:1-22
Focal Passage: 2 Chronicles 7:11-22
Key Verse: 2 Chronicles 7:14

❖ *Significance of the Lesson*

• The *Theme* of the lesson is that God hears and answers the prayers of His people when they pray in humility.

• The *Life Question* this lesson seeks to address is, When will God hear and answer my prayers?

• The *Biblical Truth* is that God hears and answers the prayers of His people when they humbly turn from their sins and seek Him.

• The *Life Impact* is to help you experience God's blessings by humbly turning from sin and seeking Him.

When Does God Answer Prayer?

In a secular worldview, people want immediate gratification of their desires. Some even expect instant answers to their prayers, and when nothing happens, they wonder whether God heard them. Some fail to see the connection between their sinful ways and their failure to experience God's blessings.

In a biblical worldview, God answers prayers, but He does so in His time and on His terms. He expects people to humbly repent of their sins. He expects those who are forgiven to continue to live within His will.

Relation to the Prayer of Jabez

During this five-week study on prayer, the topics have related to parts of Jabez's prayer in the Old Testament. This final lesson in the series relates to God's response: "And God granted him that which he requested" (1 Chron. 4:10).

Word Study: *humble*

The Hebrew word *kana* means “to subdue” or “to humble” when the subject does the acting. When the subject is acted upon, it means “to be subdued” or “to be humbled.” Often the word is used of people humbling themselves. This is the meaning in 2 Chronicles 7:14. The word is the opposite of being proud. To be humble is to set aside the kind of pride that causes people to think they can get along without God and to entrust themselves to God and His mercy and grace.

❖ *Search the Scriptures*

As part of the dedication of the temple, Solomon prayed a long prayer (2 Chron. 6:14-42). God’s answer to Solomon’s prayer came 13 years later. It is found in 2 Chronicles 7:11-22. In His response, God promised to answer the prayers of those who pray in humble repentance. And He warned that turning to sin would result in serious punishment.

The word “when” in the Life Question is used in two ways in this lesson. One meaning is, “When in time will God answer my prayers?” The other meaning is, “Under what conditions will God answer my prayers?” The first point in the lesson outline addresses the former of these, and the other two points address the latter.

In His Time (2 Chron. 7:11-12)

Does God answer prayer? Why does He sometimes seem to delay? Why does the Bible call for us to keep on praying? What takes the place of the sacrificial system?

Verses 11-12: **Thus Solomon finished the house of the LORD, and the king’s house: and all that came into Solomon’s heart to make in the house of the LORD, and in his own house, he prosperously effected. 12And the LORD appeared to Solomon by night, and said unto him, I have heard thy prayer, and have chosen this place to myself for an house of sacrifice.**

The Lord’s words **I have heard thy prayer** remind us that the key factor in faith is that God answers prayer. Those who believe in prayer believe in a God who answers prayer. Those who do not believe in prayer usually deny or doubt God’s existence.

Much of the skepticism about prayer is based on false views of what people expect it to be. Many think of prayer as only an alternative method of getting something they want. Some think of God as being like the genie in the story of Aladdin and his lamp. When God doesn't respond immediately, or even later, they assume that He does not answer prayers. Someone has said that God always answers prayer, but His answer may be yes, no, or later.

Verses 11-12 give one of many Bible examples of answers to prayers that seem to have been delayed. At the temple's dedication, Solomon had asked God for some specific things about the temple (6:14-42). God gave an immediate sign of His basic approval by sending fire to consume the sacrifices (7:1), but a more definitive answer did not come at that time.

Verse 11 states that **Solomon finished the house of the Lord, and the king's house.** These were two separate building projects. First Kings 7:1 says that the construction of the palace took 13 years. This was following the completion of the temple, which took 7 years to build (1 Kings 6:38; 9:10). First Kings 9:1-2 records the same appearance of the Lord to Solomon as is described here in 2 Chronicles 7:11-12. This is called "the second time" that the Lord appeared to Solomon, the first being at Gibeon when the Lord had promised to give the new king whatever he asked (1 Kings 3:3-15). Both appearances were **by night.** Thus 13 years passed between the prayer of dedication and the Lord's answer. "In spite of the close proximity of Solomon's prayer to this second appearance of God in the text, both Kings and Chronicles separate the two events. In fact, it took some thirteen years to accomplish this double task."[1]

God answers some prayers during or shortly after the prayer. Hannah prayed for a son and soon became pregnant, and in her time she gave birth to Samuel (1 Sam. 1). By contrast, Elizabeth and Zechariah asked for a child for many years, but only in their old age was John the Baptist born (Luke 1:5-25). When answers to prayers are delayed, this tests the faith of those who prayed. For example, Habakkuk prayed, "O Lord, how long shall I cry, and thou wilt not hear!" (Hab. 1:2).

God often does not explain delays in answering some prayers. We know it is not because He is too busy to get to them right away. He is not like a doctor with so many patients that a sick person must wait for a long time for the doctor to have time to see the patient. He is

Almighty God, so He is able to hear and answer whenever He chooses. Why then does He sometimes delay? For one thing, God operates on His own schedule, not on ours. What seem like delays to time-bound humans are not delays in the schedule of the eternal God.

Sometimes the one who prays does not live to see the answer. God's purposes are longer than the span of one life. Moses prayed to be able to enter the promised land. He was not allowed to do this, but the people whom he had led entered and conquered the land. David prayed to be able to build the temple. He was not allowed to do this, but he gathered materials for his son to build the temple.

Thus sometimes God delays to answer a prayer because the time is not right. Sometimes this is because of the need for the one praying to become mature enough to deal with the answer to the prayer. Many times we never know why God delays. The reason for the delay of 13 years in answering Solomon's prayer is not given. The important thing is that the prayer was heard and answered in God's time and in His way. We must trust God's wisdom and love in answering our prayers.

I . . . have chosen this place to myself for a house of sacrifice reminds us that the idea for a temple did not grow out of the dreams of David, for God had foretold such a place (Deut. 12:5). God used David, and then even more so Solomon, to get the work going—but it was according to the plan of God. The Lord established the sacrificial system of the Old Testament. It bore witness to human sins and to God's willingness to forgive repentant sinners. Christians believe that the old sacrificial system was fulfilled in Jesus Christ, who is the great High Priest and once-for-all, all-sufficient sacrifice for sin. We no longer have a temple offering animal sacrifices. We have One through whom we can "come boldly unto the throne of grace, that we may obtain mercy, and find grace to help in time of need" (Heb. 4:16). The point for us is that God's grace makes prayer possible.

What are the lasting lessons of verses 11-12?

1. God answers prayer.
2. From the human perspective of time, some answers seem slow in coming.
3. God answers prayer in His own time and in His own way.
4. We should keep on praying even when answers do not come.
5. God's grace makes prayer possible.

On His Terms (2 Chron. 7:13-16)

What part of Solomon's prayer is answered in verse 13? Why is verse 14 so familiar to many Christians? How does it relate to our world today? How do verses 15-16 apply to Christians?

Verses 13-14: **If I shut up heaven that there be no rain, or if I command the locusts to devour the land, or if I send pestilence among my people; [14]if my people, which are called by my name, shall humble themselves, and pray, and seek my face, and turn from their wicked ways; then will I hear from heaven, and will forgive their sin, and will heal their land.**

A large part of Solomon's prayer had been devoted to asking God to hear the prayers offered in the temple or toward it. Solomon acknowledged that God was too great to be confined to a temple, but because His presence was there, the temple came to represent His hearing and answering prayers (6:18-21). Then Solomon listed a number of specific situations in which prayers would be offered (vv. 22-31). God's response in 7:13 lists three of these from 6:26,28. God mentioned drought because of **no rain,** famine because of **locusts,** and **pestilence.** No doubt He intended these only as examples. The assumption is that many of these were judgments of God because of sins and that the people needed to be forgiven. Thus the prayers would focus on confession of sins.

This assumption is confirmed by 7:14. This is probably the most familiar verse in 2 Chronicles. Many of us in the evangelical tradition have heard countless sermons on this text in connection with church revivals and prayers for national or world revival. It was addressed to hearers God spoke of as **my people, which are called by my name.** God called on His people to **humble themselves.** "God resisteth the proud, but giveth grace unto the humble" (Jas. 4:6). Selfish pride is the heart of human sin. Pride assumes that we can get along without God. Humility recognizes how desperately we need God and His grace. God called for His people to **pray.** James 4:2-3 identifies two faults of many people's prayer life. One is that they do not pray. The other is that they pray only selfish prayers. A television personality was being interviewed about his problems with addiction. When he was asked how he had overcome the powerful addictions, he said that he prayed to the God of his childhood. The encouraging thing is that he prayed; the sad thing was that he had to go back to his childhood for any personal relation with God.

Seek my face means to seek God and His gracious presence. The most important result of any prayer is a closer walk with the Lord. The final necessary component of prayers of confession is for the people to **turn from their wicked ways. Turn** is the word *shub,* which means "to turn" or "to repent." Repentance is turning from sin and turning to God. These go together.

These four actions are God's terms for answering prayers of confession. God promised that when this was done, He would **hear from heaven, and will forgive their sin, and will heal their land.** In the Bible to **hear** is to heed. **Forgive** translates *salah,* the same word in Daniel 9:19. Forgiveness is removing sin as a barrier to fellowship with God. It is different from indulgence. God does not say, "Sin isn't so bad. Just forget it." He knows that real forgiveness is always costly to the one who forgives. This is one lesson that the sacrificial system was supposed to teach. God paid the price for our forgiveness at the cross. The word **heal** in the Old Testament is used of physical healing from disease and of spiritual healing from sin. **Heal their land** includes not only their forgiveness but also their restoration. It includes healing the land itself of the inevitable curses brought on it by sin.

Our nation desperately needs moral and spiritual revival. The old formula is as relevant today as it ever was. If God's people were to do what this says, such renewal would begin. Imagine what would happen if Christian people were to honestly confess and forsake their sins. What a change there would be in our lives, in our homes, in our churches, and in our land. Our land is sin-sick, and God stands ready to heal.

Verses 15-16: **Now mine eyes shall be open, and mine ears attent unto the prayer that is made in this place. 16For now have I chosen and sanctified this house, that my name may be there forever: and mine eyes and mine heart shall be there perpetually.**

Mine eyes shall be open, and mine ears attent in verse 15 is an answer to 6:40. God promised to see, and He promised to hear prayers offered in the temple. The temple signified the presence of God in and among His people. Solomon recognized that the God of heaven and earth could not be confined to a building or to any one time or place, but he asked God to abide with them in a special way in His temple. God promised to do this. The Lord said, **I have chosen and sanctified this house.** His **name** represents His presence. His **eyes** and His **heart** show His personal involvement. In the Old Testament, the Jews prayed in or toward the temple because this was the same as praying to the Lord.

The temple was destroyed in A.D. 70. Where is the presence of God to whom Christians pray? We pray to the Heavenly Father through His Son and by His Spirit, who abides in us and enables us to pray (Eph. 2:18; Rom. 8:26-27). Jesus taught us to have a private place where daily prayers are made (Matt. 6:6). He also taught that where two or three are gathered together in His name, He is present and will hear and answer their prayers (18:19-20).

God answers humble prayers, but He answers them on His own terms. Second Chronicles 7:14 states some of His terms. Others include that prayers must be prayed in faith (Matt. 21:22) and that prayer must be in accordance with God's will (1 John 5:14). These two go together. They call for us to pray to the God who is able to do all things, but to believe not only in His power to act but also to trust His wisdom and love in answering the prayer in His own way. He is our Heavenly Father. He will withhold nothing good that His children need, but He will withhold what is potentially harmful or useless.

Commenting on verses 13-16, Martin J. Selman wrote, "This paragraph reveals the heart of the books of Chronicles, and is actually Chronicles' summary of the essential message of the Old Testament."[2]

What are the lasting lessons of verses 13-16?

1. God hears and answers humble prayers of repentance.
2. Such prayers of confession must be in all our prayers.
3. Prayers of humble repentance prompt God to forgive and to heal people and land.
4. God answers sincere prayers on His own terms.

With Obedience Expected (2 Chron. 7:17-22)

Will God hear a sinner's prayer? Why is true prayer obedient to God? Why is presumption dangerous?

Verses 17-22: **And as for thee, if thou wilt walk before me, as David thy father walked, and do according to all that I have commanded thee, and shalt observe my statutes and my judgments;**
18then will I stablish the throne of thy kingdom, according as I have covenanted with David thy father, saying, There shall not fail thee a man to be ruler in Israel.
19But if ye turn away, and forsake my statutes and my commandments, which I have set before you, and

shall go and serve other gods, and worship them; [20]then will I pluck them up by the roots out of my land which I have given them; and this house, which I have sanctified for my name, will I cast out of my sight, and will make it to be a proverb and a byword among all nations. [21]And this house, which is high, shall be an astonishment to every one that passeth by it; so that he shall say, Why hath the LORD done thus unto this land, and unto this house? [22]And it shall be answered, Because they forsook the LORD God of their fathers, which brought them forth out of the land of Egypt, and laid hold on other gods, and worshiped them, and served them: therefore hath he brought all this evil upon them.

Verses 17-18 were addressed to Solomon. **Thou** is singular here, but **ye** in verse 19 is plural, referring to all the people. God's word to Solomon was a reaffirmation of His promise to David that one of his descendants would reign forever. This promise was not fulfilled in Solomon or any of the other kings of David's line, but in Jesus, the son of David and the Son of God.

Verse 17 shows what God expected of Solomon. God expects the same of all who pray to Him. We must **walk before** Him **and do according to all that** He has **commanded.** God promised to bless Solomon as one of David's heirs of God's promise to David. This means that prayer must be accompanied by an obedient life. Sometimes people ask, "Will God answer a sinner's prayer?" The answer must be twofold. For one thing, since all of us are sinners, the only prayers are sinners' prayers (2 Chron. 6:36). God hears the sincere prayers of sincere, repentant sinners. On the other hand, God will not hear the prayers of people who continue in their sins and presume on God's forgiveness.

> If I had cherished sin in my heart,
> the Lord would not have listened;
> but God has surely listened
> and heard my voice in prayer (Ps. 66:18-19, NIV).

Verses 19-22 contain a warning to Solomon and to all the people. God warned them of what would happen if they turned away, forsook God's commandments, and worshiped other gods. If they did these things, God would **pluck them up by the roots out of my land.** The holy temple, which God was accepting as a place for worship and prayers, would be destroyed. In fact, it would become a place of such desolation that people would wonder what happened. The answer would be that the people whom God delivered from Egypt had turned from the Lord, and He had punished them for their persistent rejection. Unfortunately, that is exactly what happened.

The temple ceased to be a place for people to confess their sins and to go forth to live for the Lord. The prayers became hypocritical prayers because people tried to use the temple worship as a shield for their sins. The prophets thundered away at such false worship and prayers. Amos said that the Lord hated such hypocrisy (Amos 5:21-24). Isaiah declared in God's name, "When ye spread forth your hands, I will hide mine eyes from you: yea, when ye make many prayers, I will not hear: your hands are full of blood" (Isa. 1:15). In Jeremiah's day, the people had developed a doctrine that God would never allow His temple or His people to fall into the hands of an enemy. Speaking through Jeremiah, God asked, "Will ye steal, murder, and commit adultery, and swear falsely, and burn incense unto Baal, and walk after other gods whom ye know not; and come and stand before me in this house, which is called by my name, and say, We are delivered to do all these abominations?" (Jer. 7:9-10).

King Claudius was the villain in Shakespeare's *Hamlet.* He had murdered his brother the king and taken his throne and his wife. He went into the chapel and tried to pray. But he found that he could not pray since he intended to retain his crown and his wife, both the fruits of his evil actions. He could not truly repent of sins that he intended to hold on to. Sadly he concluded,

> My words fly up, my thoughts remain below:
> Words without thoughts never to heaven go.[3]

What are the lasting lessons in verses 17-22?

1. God expects obedience from those who pray.
2. He blesses such obedience.
3. He warns of disobedience.
4. He will punish the sin of disobedience and not hear the prayers of hypocrites.

❖ *Spiritual Transformations*

When does God hear our prayers? His answer to Solomon's prayer came 13 years after the prayer was made. God answers prayer in His own time. God promised to hear prayers of humble repentance prayed in or toward the temple. He answers prayers on His own terms. God calls for obedience and warns of the consequences of disobedience. God expects obedience from those who pray.

What have been your experiences and observations about when and how God answers prayer? ______________________________

What characteristics of true prayer do you need to begin to practice or strengthen? ______________________________

Prayer of Commitment: Lord, help me to trust and obey You even when my prayer does not seem to be answered. Amen.

[1]J. A. Thompson, "1,2 Chronicles," in *The New American Commentary,* vol. 9 [Nashville: Broadman & Holman Publishers, 1994], 235.

[2]Martin J. Selman, *2 Chronicles,* in the Tyndale Old Testament Commentaries [Downers Grove: InterVarsity Press, 1994], 337.

[3]William Shakespeare, *Hamlet,* Act III, section 4.

Study Theme

Who Are You, Jesus?

"Who is this?" This question was often asked about Jesus (Matt. 21:10; Luke 5:21; 7:49; 9:9). Jesus asked His disciples who people said He was, and He asked them who they thought He was (Matt. 16:13-15; Mark 8:27-29; Luke 9:18-20). Jesus helped answer this question by seven "I am" statements, which are found in John's Gospel:

- "I am the bread of life" (6:35,48).
- "I am the light of the world" (8:12; 9:5).
- "I am the door" (10:7,9).
- "I am the good shepherd" (10:11,14).
- "I am the resurrection, and the life" (11:25).
- "I am the way, the truth, and the life" (14:6).
- "I am the vine" (15:1,5).

When God called Moses to be the human leader through whom God delivered Israel from Egyptian slavery, Moses asked God to tell him His name. God replied that "I AM" was His name (Ex. 3:14). By using "I am," Jesus was claiming to be Deity. Christianity is not primarily a way of life, a set of beliefs, or a mystical experience. It is the person of Jesus Christ.

This Study Theme focuses on who Jesus is and how God's grace is demonstrated to humanity through Jesus' purpose, love, resurrection, and provision. The Gospel of John emphasizes Jesus' unique nature and mission as "the One and Only, who came from the Father, full of grace and truth" (1:14, NIV). Four of the "I am" statements are the basis for the four lessons in this study. These are "the light of the world," "the good shepherd," "the resurrection and the life," and "the bread of life." April 20 is the Easter Coordinated Evangelism Lesson for older children, youth, and adults.

This study theme is designed to help you

- testify through your faith and worship that Jesus is God (Apr. 6)
- appreciate and strengthen your relationship with Jesus Christ (Apr. 13)
- live confidently as a believer in view of Christ's promise of resurrection and eternal life (Apr. 20)
- trust Jesus daily to provide for your needs (Apr. 27)

Week of April 6

THE LIGHT OF THE WORLD

Background Passage: John 8:12; 9:1-41
Focal Passage: John 8:12; 9:1-7,35-41
Key Verse: John 8:12

❖ *Significance of the Lesson*

• The *Theme* of the lesson is that Jesus reveals His purpose.

• The *Life Question* this lesson seeks to address is, Why should I believe that Jesus is truly God?

• The *Biblical Truth* is that Jesus is God, and He summons people to believe in Him as the One who reveals the truth and gives them life.

• The *Life Impact* is to help you testify through your life and worship that Jesus is God.

Is Jesus God?

In non-Christian worldviews, Jesus is viewed at best as the human founder of one of the world's major religions. The New Testament accounts of His life, ministry, death, and resurrection are viewed either as false or as irrelevant to modern life. For some people, *Jesus* is only a swear word.

In the biblical worldview, Jesus is the divine Son of God who became fully human while retaining His full deity. He calls people to follow Him as Savior and Lord, and He is worthy of believers' sincere worship.

Word Study: *believe*

The verb *pisteuo* is found many times throughout John's Gospel. It is usually translated "believe." However, since our English word *believe* often means only to accept something as true, we need to recognize that the biblical word refers to more than mental acceptance of the true facts about Jesus. It has the idea of personal commitment and trust.

❖ *Search the Scriptures*

Jesus declared that He is the Light of the world. He healed a man born blind. When the Pharisees cast this man out, Jesus found him and the man professed faith in Jesus and worshiped Him. Jesus told the Pharisees that He had come to give sight to the blind and to cause those who see to become blind.

The four points in the Focal Passage Outline provide answers to the Life Question, Why should I believe that Jesus is truly God?

Jesus Dispels Life's Darkness (John 8:12)

In what ways is this verse a claim to deity by Jesus? How is the title ***the light of the world*** *similar to the title "the Savior of the world"? What must people do to experience this light?*

John 8:12: **Then spake Jesus again unto them, saying, I am the light of the world: he that followeth me shall not walk in darkness, but shall have the light of life.**

Many Bible students believe that this verse continues the biblical account of what happened during the Feast of Tabernacles described in John 7. John 7:37 reflects one of the rituals of that feast, and John 8:12 reflects another. One of the rituals had to do with water and the other with light. Water was carried from the Pool of Siloam and poured into a funnel beside the altar of sacrifice. On the last day of the feast, "Jesus stood and cried, saying, If any man thirst, let him come unto me, and drink" (7:37). Another ritual was the lighting of golden lamps in the temple. We cannot conceive of how dark nights were before modern ways of illumination. This bright display of light was striking as it pierced the darkness. Jesus was probably using that ceremony as a background to His claim to be **the light of the world.** To claim to be **the light** is a divine claim. The Scripture states that God clothes Himself with light, dwells in light, and is the light (Ps. 104:2; Dan. 2:22; 1 John 1:5).

The Feast of Tabernacles reminded the people of their experiences on the way to the promised land. The water reminded them that God gave them water from a rock. The lights reminded them of the pillar of fire. The pillar of fire signified the presence of God among His people (Ex. 13:21-22).

Both **light** and the pillar of fire were also symbols of divine deliverance or salvation: "The LORD is my light and my salvation" (Ps. 27:1). The pillar of fire stood between the pursuing Egyptians and the

Israelites in Exodus 14:19-20. Light in the Bible is set over against **darkness,** which signifies sin or evil. We see this in passages such as John 3:17-21 and many others. Thus Jesus is **the light** in the sense of saving from the darkness of sin. As Peter wrote: He "called you out of darkness into his marvelous light" (1 Pet. 2:9).

Don't overlook the words **of the world.** Jesus claimed to be the divine Son of God who is also "the Savior of the world" (John 4:42).

The benefits of the Light of the world are not automatic. People must follow Jesus in order to be promised that they **shall not walk in darkness, but shall have the light of life. The light of life** can mean "light is life" or "life comes from light." Either way, those who follow **the light of the world** find the life that only Christ can bring. **Life** is one of the themes of the Gospel of John. The word refers not only to physical life but also to abundant and eternal life in Christ. This life means a transformed life and a life in right relation to God.

Jesus is the Light of the world who dispels the darkness in the lives of those who follow Him. Philip P. Bliss had John 8:12 and chapter 9 in mind when he wrote the hymn "The Light of the World Is Jesus."

The whole world was lost in the darkness of sin,
  The Light of the world is Jesus;
Like sunshine at noonday His glory shone in,
  The Light of the world is Jesus.
Come to the Light, 'tis shining for thee;
Sweetly the Light has dawned upon me,
Once I was blind, but now I can see:
  The Light of the world is Jesus.[1]

What are the lasting lessons in John 8:12?

1. As the Light of the world, Jesus is the divine Son of God.
2. Jesus is the Savior of the world.
3. Jesus dispels the darkness of sin from the lives of those who follow Him.
4. Jesus gives life to those who follow Him.

Jesus Does God's Work (John 9:1-7)

*What was the disciples' view of the relation of suffering and sin? What was Jesus' view? What did Jesus mean by **the works of God**? Why did Jesus put something on the man's eyes and tell him to wash in the pool of Siloam?*

John 9:1-5: **And as Jesus passed by, he saw a man which was blind from his birth. [2]And his disciples asked him, saying, Master, who did sin, this man, or his parents, that he was born blind? [3]Jesus answered, Neither hath this man sinned, nor his parents: but that the works of God should be made manifest in him. [4]I must work the works of him that sent me, while it is day: the night cometh, when no man can work. [5]As long as I am in the world, I am the light of the world.**

The Bible does not tell the exact setting of this incident. However, the repetition of **I am the light of the world** in verse 5 shows that the story of chapter 9 illustrates the saying of John 8:12.

Jesus always **saw** people through eyes of compassion. The **man which was blind from his birth** was probably well known in the area. Jesus saw the man as one who needed the work of divine healing. The disciples saw him as a pitiful case, one about whom to discuss the theological meaning of the relation of sin and suffering. In spite of the Book of Job, they, along with most of their countrymen, thought that such a disability must be punishment for sin. The most likely explanation, they thought, was that **he was born blind** because of some sin of his parents. But some of the Jews believed that a preborn child in the womb could commit sin. They used the example of Esau within Rebekah's womb (Gen. 25:22-23). Thus when the disciples saw the man, they asked, **Who did sin, this man, or his parents, that he was born blind?** They assumed that it was one or the other.

The Book of Job clearly shows that all suffering is not the direct result of someone's sin. Jesus took the same position with the man born blind. This does not mean that sin never causes suffering. Jesus' words to the crippled man in the temple imply that his malady was related to his sin (John 5:14). But this was not true of the man born blind. **Jesus answered, Neither hath this man sinned, nor his parents.** Jesus did not mean that they were sinless, but He refused to connect their sins to the man's blindness.

Jesus' explanation is stated in verses 3b-4. One interpretation of these words is that God caused the man to be born blind so that Jesus could heal Him. F. F. Bruce offered an alternate view, however: "This does not mean that God deliberately caused the child to be born blind in order that, after many years, his glory should be displayed in the removal of the blindness. . . . It does mean that God overruled the disaster of the child's blindness so that, when the child grew to manhood, he might, by recovering his sight, see the glory of God in the face of Christ, and others, seeing this work of God, might turn to the true Light of the World."[2]

To put it another way, the disciples wanted to speculate about the cause of the man's blindness; Jesus focused on acting to cure the man. Herschel H. Hobbs proposed a translation of verses 3-5 that emphasized the cure rather than the cause. Hobbs noted that the Greek writings of the first century had only one kind of punctuation mark—the question mark (which looked like our semi-colon). He proposed the following translation by moving the period: "Neither this man sinned, nor his parents. But that the works of God should be made manifest in him, we must work the works of Him that sent me while it is day: the night comes when no man can work. As long as I am in the world, I am the light of the world."[3]

One of the key words in verses 3-4 is the noun **works** and the verb **work.** Jesus came to do the works of God, which called for action, not speculation. God was at work through Him to meet human needs. The word **must** showed the urgency of doing the works of God when opportunity presented itself. Jesus was committed to acting **while it is day** because **the night cometh, when no man can work.** Jesus knew that His earthly ministry was drawing to a close. He wanted to take advantage of the time remaining. This principle applies to all of us. In fact, based on different manuscripts, many translators have "we" (NRSV, HCSB) instead of **I** at the beginning of verse 4. Either way, the principle is valid for Jesus and for His followers. Life is short and uncertain. We often cross paths with someone only once; we should allow God to work through us to witness or minister to that person while we have the opportunity. Verse 5 then shows how Jesus applied this principle to Himself: "While I am in the world, I am the light of the world" (NIV).

John 9:6-7: **When he had thus spoken, he spat on the ground, and made clay of the spittle, and he anointed the eyes of the blind man with the clay, 7and said unto him, Go wash in the pool of Siloam, (which is by interpretation, Sent). He went his way therefore, and washed, and came seeing.**

In the Old Testament, the giving of sight is often associated with the Messiah (Isa. 29:18; 35:5; 42:7). Jesus claimed to be the fulfillment of one such passage (Luke 4:18). The Gospels record many occasions when Jesus physically opened the eyes of the blind (Matt. 9:27-31; 12:22-28; 15:30-31; 21:14; Mark 8:22-26; Luke 7:21-22).

John 9 tells of the only time that it is specifically stated Jesus healed a man born blind.

Jesus **anointed** the man's eyes with a mixture of **clay** and **spittle.** He told the man, **Go wash in the pool of Siloam.** When Jesus healed blind Bartimaeus, He simply spoke the word (Mark 10:46-52). Why did Jesus not simply speak the word in John 9? The Bible does not explain why Jesus used the clay and washing in healing the man born blind. Leon Morris wrote: "It is known that the ancient world often attributed curative powers to saliva. And it may have helped this particular man to have something he might do himself" by going and washing.[4] The use of mud and water does not diminish the miracle. The man clearly considered his sight as a miracle wrought by Jesus (v. 11).

The command to **Go wash in the pool of Siloam** gave the blind man an opportunity to exercise his faith. Elisha told Naaman to dip himself seven times in the Jordan River. The proud Syrian almost missed his opportunity; but he finally obeyed, and he emerged cleansed of his leprosy (2 Kings 5:9-14). Unlike Naaman, no one had to persuade the blind man to obey Jesus. When he **washed,** he **came seeing.** This kind of quick obedience and faith was true of the man throughout John 9.

What are the lasting lessons of John 9:1-7?

1. Suffering is not always the direct result of sin.
2. Rather than speculating about the cause of the plight of needy people, we should act to help them.
3. Allow God to do His work though you.
4. Use each opportunity to help others because life is short and uncertain.
5. Do what Jesus tells you to do.

Jesus Summons Belief (John 9:35-38)

*From what was the man cast out? What is the significance of the word **found**? How did Jesus reveal Himself to the man? What were the steps the man took in moving toward full faith?*

John 9:35-38: **Jesus heard that they had cast him out; and when he had found him, he said unto him, Dost thou believe on the Son of God? 36He answered and said, Who is he, Lord, that I might believe on him? 37And Jesus said unto him, Thou hast both seen him, and it is he that talketh with thee. 38And he said, Lord, I believe. And he worshiped him.**

The Pharisees had **cast him out.** This could mean that they threw him out of where they were meeting, but it seems to have been more serious. Earlier his parents had been careful what they said to the Pharisees because they feared that they would be "put out of the synagogue" (v. 22). Later Jewish writings reveal that there were several levels of discipline. The most serious of these was expulsion from the synagogue. This was like being treated by the entire community as if the person were dead.

The words **found him** remind us of Jesus' mission to seek and to save the lost (Luke 19:10). So when John wrote that Jesus **found** the man, he meant more than locating him. Jesus found him as part of His mission to bring the man to light and salvation.

The question **Dost thou believe on the Son of God?** was designed to lead the man to full faith. Some translations have "Son of man" (NIV, HCSB). Both titles point to the full deity and humanity of Jesus.

The man's response in verse 36 shows his openness and eagerness to believe. Throughout the events of John 9 the man responded positively to each new bit of light as he received it. He walked in the light he had and moved forward each time he received more light.

As soon as Jesus told the man that He was the Son of God, the man said, **Lord, I believe.** He made an immediate profession of his faith in Jesus as the Son of God. "Here believing did not mean the mere acceptance of signs (cf. 2:23-25) but the active commitment of himself to the Son of Man, who brought God's hope and forgiveness to the world."[5]

The man also **worshiped** Jesus. This is one of the marks of true faith. When the healed man remembered what Jesus had done for him, his heart overflowed with joy and gratitude. This was expressed in worship.

Review the steps in the man's pilgrimage from darkness to light. He constantly moved toward the light and let nothing stop him. First, he obeyed Jesus' voice to wash his eyes. When his neighbors asked him who had healed him, he told all he knew at the time by calling Jesus the man who had healed him. When the Pharisees first tried to pressure him to deny Jesus, he said that Jesus was a prophet. Later he refused to be moved from the fact that once he was blind but now he could see. During the final confrontation with the Pharisees, he said that Jesus was a man from God. When Jesus fully revealed Himself as the Son of God, the man believed and worshiped the Lord.

What are the lasting lessons of John 9:35-38?
1. Enemies of Christ persecute true followers.
2. Jesus seeks sinners in order to save them.
3. Saving faith requires personal commitment.
4. One expression of true faith in Jesus is to worship Him.

Jesus Judges Unbelief (John 9:39-41)

How can we reconcile verse 39 with John 3:16-17? What part of verse 39 does the blind man illustrate? What part of the verse do the Pharisees illustrate? In what sense were the Pharisees able to see? In what sense were they blind?

John 9:39-41: **And Jesus said, For judgment I am come into this world, that they which see not might see; and that they which see might be made blind. 40And some of the Pharisees which were with him heard these words, and said unto him, Are we blind also? 41Jesus said unto them, If ye were blind, ye should have no sin: but now ye say, We see; therefore your sin remaineth.**

On the surface verse 39 seems to contradict John 3:16-17. In John 3:16-17 Jesus said that He had come to save, not to judge. Yet in John 9:39 He said, **For judgment I am come into this world.** No conflict exists if we read 3:18-21 with verses 16-17. Jesus came to save from sin, but He can save only those who turn to Him in faith. Those who reject Him through unbelief choose darkness rather than light and thus bring judgment on themselves.

Verse 39 explains the miraculous sign of John 9. The meaning of the healing of the man born blind is that Jesus is the Light of the world who offers spiritual and eternal life to all who believe. Jesus came **that they which see not might see.** The healing and saving faith of the man born blind illustrate this good news. But Jesus also came **that they which see might be made blind.** The Pharisees' persistent rejection of the light illustrates these words.

Some of the Pharisees overheard Jesus' words to the man. They asked, **Are we blind also?** Because the answer is yes and no, Jesus was careful how He answered this question. In effect He said they were not blind in the sense of being unable to see the light. If they had never been able to see the light, they would not have been accountable for rejecting the light. In other words, they would **have no sin.** Jesus, however, pointed out that they said, **We see.** As a result of being able to distinguish truth from evil, they were accountable for choosing evil. And thus Jesus announced, **Therefore your sin remaineth.** They had been able to see God's light in Christ, but they closed their eyes against the light. As a result, they lived and walked in darkness. In this sense, they were like the fish that live in the dark waters under Mammoth Cave, Kentucky. They have eyes that once could see but now are blind from living so long in the dark.

While the blind man was moving step by step toward full light, the Pharisees were moving deeper into spiritual darkness. Verse 41 does not deny that they were the spiritually blind of the final part of verse 39. Verse 41 stresses that they were accountable for becoming blind. They saw the light and truth in Jesus, but they chose to reject Him. Their persistent rejection sealed their condemnation.

In his story "The Country of the Blind," H. G. Wells told of a traveler who found himself in a valley completely cut off from the outside world. All of the inhabitants of the valley were blind. Judged by their standards, the traveler was strange. His words about "eyes" and "seeing" caused great consternation and even some hostility. Some of the leaders decided that he could never be normal until surgery removed his eyes. Meanwhile the traveler had fallen in love with a sightless girl, and she pled with him to join her in her blindness. The man refused. He escaped the country of the blind and returned to the world of light and sight.[6]

Although Mr. Wells probably intended no biblical analogy in his story, a Christian can see in this story a parable of the coming of Christ into the world. The Light of the world came into our world of darkness and sin. In blind hostility, men wanted to extinguish Him and the light. The world rejected and killed Him. But as John 1:5 says,

> The light keeps shining
> in the dark,
> and the darkness has never
> put it out (CEV).

In fact, not only is the world unable to put out the light, but the Light of the world is able to bring sight and light to many who walk in darkness.

What are the lasting lessons of John 9:39-41?

1. Jesus came to save, but those who reject Him choose judgment.
2. He is able to bring light and sight to those who believe.
3. He warns those who reject Him of their condemnation.

❖ *Spiritual Transformations*

Why should you believe in Jesus as the Light of the world and the Son of God? The Bible tells us that this is who He is. The experience of believers is that He delivers believers from the darkness of sin into eternal life. Jesus calls us to believe in Him. He warns that rejection of Him leads to condemnation.

Which of the people or groups in John 9 is closest to your experience? Do you, like the man born blind, believe in and worship Jesus as the Son of God? Have you, like the Pharisees, rejected the Light of the world? Do you, like Jesus, see people as persons to love and help? Do you, like the disciples, see needy people as hopeless cases?

How would you tell an unbeliever why you believe in Jesus as the Son of God?

What forms does your worship of Jesus take?

Prayer of Commitment: Lord Jesus, help me to bear testimony to my faith in You and to express my worship of You. Amen.

[1]*Baptist Hymnal* [Nashville: Convention Press, 1956], No. 88.

[2]F. F. Bruce, *The Gospel of John* [England: Pickering Paperbacks, 1983], 209.

[3]Herschel H. Hobbs, *The Gospel of John: Invitation to Life* [Nashville: Convention Press, 1988], 58.

[4]Leon Morris, *The Gospel According to John*, in The New International Commentary on the New Testament [Grand Rapids: William B. Eerdmans Publishing Company, 1971], 480.

[5]Gerald L. Borchert, "John 1–11," in *The New American Commentary*, vol. 25A [Nashville: Broadman & Holman Publishers, 1996], 324.

[6]H. G. Wells, *The Complete Short Stories of H. G. Wells* [New York: St. Martin's Press, Inc., 1974], 167-192.

Week of April 13

THE GOOD SHEPHERD

Background Passage: John 10:1-42
Focal Passage: John 10:11-16,22-30
Key Verse: John 10:11

❖ *Significance of the Lesson*

• The *Theme* of the lesson is that Jesus demonstrates His love.

• The *Life Question* addressed in this lesson is, How can I know that Jesus loves me?

• The *Biblical Truth* is that Jesus' willing self-sacrifice and unending care for His followers show how much He loves them.

• The *Life Impact* is to help you appreciate and strengthen your relationship with Jesus Christ.

Loved or Unloved?

The prevailing secular mind-set knows little of the security that comes from an awareness of being loved by God. Many feel that God neither knows nor cares for them. They feel alone and unloved by God. This affects their ability to show love and concern for other people.

In the biblical worldview, believers have the assurance of God's love and care. This grows out of God's revelation and redemption in Jesus, His Son. Jesus gave Himself for His people. He cares for them as a shepherd does his flock. He knows each one and they know and follow Him. Out of this relation comes the assurance of eternal life.

Word Study: *shepherd*

The Greek word *poimen* is the word for shepherd. A shepherd is someone who herds and cares for sheep. Jesus used this word in describing Himself as the Good Shepherd (John 10:11). This word is translated "pastor" when referring to the church leader who is to be a faithful under-shepherd of the Good Shepherd (Eph. 4:11).

❖ *Search the Scriptures*

Jesus boldly claimed to be the Good Shepherd who would give His life for His sheep. He taught that He knew His sheep and they knew Him. He said that His own sheep followed Him. He assured believers of eternal security in the Father's hand.

How can I know that Jesus loves me? The four Focal Passage Outline points are four answers to this *Life Question.*

Jesus Gave His Life for You (John 10:11-13)

How does Jesus as the Good Shepherd fulfill the Old Testament? What does **giveth** *mean? How is the shepherd different from the hired man? What insight comes from other New Testament passages on shepherds and sheep?*

Verses 11-13: **I am the good shepherd: the good shepherd giveth his life for the sheep. 12But he that is a hireling, and not the shepherd, whose own the sheep are not, seeth the wolf coming, and leaveth the sheep, and fleeth: and the wolf catcheth them, and scattereth the sheep. 13The hireling fleeth, because he is a hireling, and careth not for the sheep.**

In the Old Testament God is often pictured as a shepherd and His people as His flock. The most familiar passage is Psalm 23. The Old Testament also describes the Messiah as a caring Shepherd (Isa. 40:11). Ezekiel 34 is one of the important background passages to John 10:1-30. The kings of Judah were supposed to be shepherds to the people. Instead, they thought only of themselves, exploited the people, and left them for the wolves. God promised to be a true shepherd and to send the Messiah to shepherd His people (Ezek. 34:23).

Many of Jesus' hearers heard His words **I am the good shepherd** in light of such passages. Jesus was claiming to be the Messiah-Shepherd described in the Scriptures. Because Jesus used the **I am** formula, this was also another claim to deity. Jesus added the Suffering Servant idea to the title when He said, **The good shepherd giveth his life for the sheep. Giveth** translates *tithemi,* which means to "lay down" or "give up" His life. The same word is used in verses 17-18 in ways that shed light on its implications. Jesus said that His life was not taken from Him, but He gave up His life on His own. His death was voluntary. He was not a martyr but a volunteer.

Being a shepherd was a risky task. At times the work was dangerous, even life-threatening. When David was tending his father's sheep, he had to battle a lion and a bear (1 Sam. 17:34-36). In Jesus' day shepherds had to defend their flocks against wild animals, especially wolves. True shepherds felt responsible for protecting the flock. Many shepherds guarded their own sheep, but sometimes a hired man was shepherd. Jesus said that a **hireling** ("hired hand," NIV; "hired man," HCSB) might run away when he saw a **wolf coming.** These people felt no obligation to risk their own lives for the sake of someone else's sheep. By fleeing before danger, the hired person left the sheep to be ravaged and scattered. Such action showed that he **careth not for the sheep.**

What are the lasting lessons in verses 11-13?

1. Jesus is the Good Shepherd, and His people are His flock.

2. Jesus voluntarily laid down His life so we might be saved and become part of His flock.

3. Those who are responsible to care for believers but abandon them at a crucial time do not really care for God's people. They care only for themselves.

Jesus Knows You Completely (John 10:14-16)

*In what sense does the Good Shepherd **know** each of His sheep? In what sense does each one know Him? Who are the **other sheep** of verse 16? How does the Good Shepherd's knowledge of His sheep show them that He loves them?*

Verses 14-15: **I am the good shepherd, and know my sheep, and am known of mine. [15]As the Father knoweth me, even so know I the Father: and I lay down my life for the sheep.**

The second emphasis about the Good Shepherd is that He knows His sheep and they know Him. Jesus compared this kind of knowledge to the way God the Father and God the Son know each other. None of us has the kind of perfect knowledge that only God can have, but this divine knowledge has some characteristics that are part of what it means to know God and to be known by Him. For one thing, it is knowledge of personal relationship, not impersonal knowledge of a thing. The Good Shepherd knows each of His sheep in a personal relationship. The same is true of our knowledge of Him. Knowledge of facts about someone is important, but personal knowledge is basic to the mutual knowledge of relationships.

This shows us two more ways that Jesus loves us. First, it shows that Jesus knows and cares for each one in a personal way. Second, it shows that Jesus allows us to know Him in a personal way. Even though God is too great for us to comprehend and to understand His ways, He invites us to know Him and to trust Him through Jesus, the Good Shepherd.

Verse 16: **And other sheep I have, which are not of this fold: them also I must bring, and they shall hear my voice; and there shall be one fold, and one shepherd.**

Jesus said that He had **other sheep** that were **not of this fold.** Jesus used the word **must** to show His intention and obligation to **bring** them also. He said, **They shall hear my voice.** The long-range plan was to have **one fold, and one shepherd.** *Aule* is the Greek word for **fold.** This word is used in verse 1 and in the first use of **fold** in verse 16. It referred to a courtyard that had walls and a door but was open to the sky, a "sheep pen" (NIV). The second word for **fold** in **there shall be one fold** in verse 16b is *poimen.* This is more properly a "flock" (NIV, HCSB). A single sheep fold or sheep pen might hold one flock or several flocks, but not necessarily all the sheep of one flock. Jesus was looking toward God's future when all His people would be together as one under the lordship of Jesus Christ. Thus the **other sheep** probably refers to Gentile believers who would be sought and found after Jesus' death and resurrection and the coming of the Spirit with power at Pentecost.

The International Mission Board of the Southern Baptist Convention is focusing on reaching unreached people groups throughout the world. Jesus has potential sheep in each of these groups. Those who take them the good news are helping the Good Shepherd find those other sheep who will constitute His one flock.

When I was growing up, the pastor of our church had a true shepherd's heart. One evidence of this is that he knew everyone's name—old and young. And this was a growing church with new members coming regularly. On one occasion all of us were standing around the walls of the church building. He went around the room and called each one by name. Because each of us knew him, we knew that his knowing our names was not just an intellectual feat or the gift of a good memory. It meant that he knew and cared about each of us.

Jesus knows each of us by name—and in every other way. Our personal relationship with Him is based on His knowledge of us and our knowledge of Him. Being known by Him and being able to know Him show us He loves us.

What are the lasting lessons of verses 14-16?

1. Jesus knows us and cares for us.
2. This is the knowledge of personal relationship.
3. Jesus' long-range objective is to make one flock of all God's people.
4. We should seek to reach others so they can be included among God's people.

Jesus Guides You Through Life (John 10:22-27)

When did this event happen? Why did the Jews ask Jesus to tell them plainly if He is the Messiah? How is unbelief shown? How is belief shown? What characteristics of shepherds in the eastern countries are seen in verse 27? What is involved in following Jesus? How do you see Jesus' love in His guidance?

Verses 22-27: **And it was at Jerusalem the feast of the dedication,
and it was winter. 23And Jesus walked in the temple in Solomon's
porch. 24Then came the Jews round about him, and said unto him,
How long dost thou make us to doubt? If thou be the Christ, tell us
plainly. 25Jesus answered them, I told you, and ye believed not: the
works that I do in my Father's name, they bear witness of me.
26But ye believe not, because ye are not of my sheep, as I said unto
you. 27My sheep hear my voice, and I know them, and they follow me.**

The events beginning with verse 22 clearly took place at **the feast of the dedication** in the **winter.** As **Jesus walked in the temple in Solomon's porch,** His critics confronted Him and asked Him to **tell** them **plainly** whether He was **the Christ,** that is, the Messiah. Jesus had been cautious among the Jews about openly claiming to be the Messiah because many of them had such distorted views about the Messiah.

Jesus told them that His **works** done **in** His **Father's name** showed who He was, but they **believed not.** He told them their unbelief showed they were not His sheep. Then He described the behavior of true believers: **My sheep hear my voice, and I know them, and they follow me.** These words recall what Jesus stated in verses 3-5, which describe some distinctive characteristics of the shepherd-sheep relationship in Jesus' day. Gerald Borchert, writing in the *New American Commentary,* explained: "Those who have lived primarily in western world settings, where shepherding is normally done by driving sheep with dogs, may find it hard to envisage the intimacy of the biblical shepherd passages. There the shepherd is pictured as having a personal attachment to the sheep, and the sheep are portrayed as recognizing the shepherd's voice and responding accordingly. Having taught in Israel, two illustrations have become seared in my memory concerning eastern shepherds and their sheep. Of the two pictures, one is that of a shepherd leading his sheep through the city of Jerusalem just outside the Jaffa Gate. Cars were whizzing by while the shepherd sang and gently whistled to his sheep, and they dutifully followed him despite all of the bustling traffic nearby. The other picture is that of an early morning with the Bedouins when the shepherds began to lead their sheep out of the sheepfold, which contained the combined flocks of four shepherds. As each shepherd took his turn and began to sing and call his sheep, they dutifully separated from the larger flock and began to follow him to the hills for their daylight feeding."[1]

Psalm 23:1-4 is good commentary on this. The Lord leads the sheep into green pastures and beside still waters. He also leads in paths of righteousness for His name's sake. But He also leads through the valley of the shadow of death. Nevertheless, He goes before His sheep and with His sheep wherever He leads.

How does the Good Shepherd's guidance show you His love? He leads you in the ways of life and joy, even through the dark valleys. We are blessed not to know our exact future in this life. We are blessed in being able to trust Him to guide us in the ways we should go and to be sufficient for each situation. As you look back on your life, can you see evidences of the guiding hand of the Good Shepherd?

Savior, like a shepherd lead us,
  Much we need Thy tender care;
In Thy pleasant pastures feed us,
  For our use Thy folds prepare.[2]

What are the lasting lessons of verses 22-27?

1. Faith is necessary to be one of Christ's sheep.
2. Those who belong to the Lord know Him and follow Him.
3. We don't know the future, but we can trust Christ to lead us and be with us.

Jesus Gives Eternal Security (John 10:28-30)

What do these verses teach about life? Why will believers ***never perish****? How does this passage teach eternal security? How does eternal security show you that Jesus loves you?*

Verses 28-29: **And I give unto them eternal life; and they shall never perish, neither shall any man pluck them out of my hand. 29My Father, which gave them me, is greater than all; and no man is able to pluck them out of my Father's hand.**

Each line in these verses is packed with meaning. **I give unto them eternal life.** Life is a gift. This is true of earthly life and it is true of spiritual life. The word *life* is found repeatedly in John's Gospel. Three of the seven "I am" statements have the word in the title: "the bread of life," "the resurrection and the life," and "the way, the truth, and the life." Jesus gives physical life as a gift to all who are born. He gives abundant and eternal life to all who are born anew of the Spirit. This life begins with the new birth and it never ends.

And they shall never perish is the negative side of the previous promise. This doesn't mean that believers will never experience physical death, but it does mean that believers will never experience the second death. "For God so loved the world, that he gave his only begotten Son, that whosoever believeth in him should not perish, but have everlasting life" (John 3:16).

Neither shall any man pluck them out of my hand. The hand of Jesus is the hand of God; therefore, verse 29 elaborates on this line from verse 28. Verse 29 shows that God **gave** the believers to the Son. The **Father . . . is greater than all.** As a result, **no man is able to pluck** believers **out of** the **Father's hand.**

People are looking for security, but they are looking in the wrong places and often for the wrong kind of security. God is the only source of lasting security. There is no better place to be than in the hand of God. This is true only for believers who entrust themselves into His hand. It is not a good place to be for those who have rejected Christ and chosen a life of sin. In their cases, being in God's hand will result in judgment. But for believers, being in God's hand means security—eternal security.

Many Bible passages support the doctrine of eternal security. This doctrine assures true believers that their salvation is eternal. This is something we can know. First John 5:11-13 reads: "And this is the record, that God hath given to us eternal life, and this life is in his Son. He that hath the Son hath life; and he that hath not the Son of God hath not life. These things have I written unto you that believe on the name of the Son of God; that ye may know that ye have eternal life. . . ." This truth is based on the grace and power of God. If we were saved by our own goodness, we could have no such assurance; however, since God saved us while we were still sinners, He can and will complete that work of salvation (Phil. 1:6).

John 10:29 bases our assurance on the power of God's hand to hold on to us and to allow nothing or no one to snatch us from God's hand. Our eternal security is not based on our ability to have a strong grasp on the hand of God with our hands. Sometimes we falter in faith or in righteousness, but His grasp never slackens. This simple parable illustrates what I mean. A father and his small son were preparing to walk on an icy sidewalk. The dad asked his son to let him hold the boy's hand, but the child insisted he could make it without help. Soon his feet flew out from under him and down he went. When he got up, his father again asked to be allowed to hold the boy's hand, but the child said he would hold onto his father's hand. Again his feet slipped on the ice and his grasp on his dad's hand was not strong enough to keep him from falling. When his father helped him up this time, the humbled child allowed the father to grasp him in his strong grip. The boy continued to slip at times, but he did not fall. He was held in a grasp stronger than his own. When we allow God to hold us in His hand, His hand never fails to hold us. His hold on us is always stronger than our hold on Him.

Verse 30: **I and my Father are one.**

This short verse supports the doctrine of the incarnation of Jesus as God's Son. Jesus was following up on what He had just said in verses 28-29. He had spoken of believers being in His hand. Then He spoke of them being in the Father's hand. To be in the hand of Jesus is to be in the hand of God because Jesus and the **Father are one.** Some people misunderstand this verse to mean that the Son and the Father are the same person, that they have no separate identities. Over the centuries Christians have carefully stated the way they speak of the incarnation and the Trinity.

The Bible speaks of one God. This one God exists in three persons—Father, Son, and Holy Spirit. We believe in God as Father, Son, and Holy Spirit for two reasons: One, this is how God has revealed Himself. Two, this is how we have experienced God. When we use the word *one,* we generally use it in a numerical sense of one thing that can be confined in one place. When we use the word *one* to describe God, we must realize that God is beyond our ability to fully understand or define. His oneness includes the God to whom we pray, the Son through whom we pray, and the Spirit who helps us pray. Thus Jesus was speaking of oneness of nature, spirit, and purpose.

Jesus, my Lord, will love me forever,
From Him no pow'r of evil can sever,
He gave His life to ransom my soul,
Now I belong to Him.[3]

What are the lasting lessons of verses 28-30?

1. Eternal life is the gift of God.
2. Believers will never perish in the second death.
3. Believers are safe and securely held in the hand of God.
4. Christians can and should know that they have eternal life.
5. Jesus and God the Father are one in nature, purpose, and spirit.
6. You can know Jesus loves you because He gives you eternal security.

❖ *Spiritual Transformations*

A renowned European theologian was traveling in the United States. He was known for his many theological writings. The people who heard him had varying opinions and understandings of his ideas. At one meeting he was asked to name the greatest theological insight he knew. He said, "Jesus loves me! This I know, for the Bible tells me so." During this study we have noted four reasons why Christians believe that Jesus loves them. *Name four reasons the Bible says that Jesus loves you.*

1.
2.
3.
4.

In what way can you appreciate and strengthen your love relationship with the Lord? ____________________

____

Prayer of Commitment: Lord Jesus, I thank You for Your great love. Help me to grow in appreciation and strength in that love. Amen.

[1]Gerald Borchert, "John 1–11," NAC, 330.
[2]Dorothy A. Thrupp, "Savior, Like a Shepherd Lead Us," No. 61, *The Baptist Hymnal*, 1991.
[3]Norman J. Clayton, "Now I Belong to Jesus," No. 345, *The Baptist Hymnal*, 1991.

Week of April 20

THE RESURRECTION AND THE LIFE

Background Passage: John 11:1-57
Focal Passage: John 11:1-4,21-27,38-40,43-44
Key Verses: John 11:25-26

❖ *Significance of the Lesson*

• The *Theme* of this lesson is that Jesus is the Resurrection and the Life.

• The *Life Question* this lesson seeks to address is, What hope do I have concerning life after death?

• The *Biblical Truth* is that because of Jesus' resurrection, those who trust in Jesus as Savior experience new life now and will be raised to live with Him forever after death.

• The *Life Impact* is to help you live confidently as a believer in view of Christ's promise of resurrection and eternal life.

• This lesson is the *Easter Coordinated Evangelism Lesson.*

Life After Death

The prevailing secular worldview considers death as final and the end of one's existence in any form. Thus any hope for or belief in life after death is unscientific, irrational, and futile. At best, adherents of the secular worldview find hope in being able to preserve their names and their memories indirectly through descendants, personal fame, or bequests. At its worst, the secular mind-set leads to a materialistic view of life that says you go around only once in life so get all you can while you can. In addition to this secular worldview are the views of life after death held by other religions and by those who have a hope based on their own goodness rather than on the grace of God. Some other religions teach a future paradise for martyrs of their cause. Some teach reincarnation and a hope for a future nirvana.

In the biblical worldview, death is a reality and the termination of physical life, but it is not the end of existence. Death is the ally of sin, and both were defeated by Jesus' death and resurrection. The final defeat of sin and death will be in the future, but believers already have the assurance of salvation from sin and victory over death. Believers can live and die with confidence of eternal life in Jesus.

Word Study: *Life, live*

In John 11:25-26 the word for "life" is *zoe,* and the related verb "live" is *zao.* Both words at times refer to physical life, but often in the Bible they refer to life in relation with God, life that is eternal. *Life* is found more often in John's Gospel than in any other Bible book (36 times). Life is something everyone wants to have, and the Bible says that Jesus Christ is the source of all true life.

❖ *Search the Scriptures*

The sickness and death of Lazarus illustrate the reality of these things for all people. The confident hope of victory over death is based on the One who is the Resurrection and the Life. Jesus' raising Lazarus from the dead foreshadowed His own unique resurrection from death.

What hope can you have of life after death? The three Focal Passage Outline headings point toward the answer to this crucial question.

Death Is a Reality for All (John 11:1-4)

What does the Bible tell us about the three people in verse 1? What message did the sisters send to Jesus? What did Jesus mean in verse 4? Where was Jesus at this time?

Verses 1-4: **Now a certain man was sick, named Lazarus, of
Bethany, the town of Mary and her sister Martha. [2](It was that Mary
which anointed the Lord with ointment, and wiped his feet with her
hair, whose brother Lazarus was sick.) [3]Therefore his sisters sent
unto him, saying, Lord, behold, he whom thou lovest is sick. [4]When
Jesus heard that, he said, This sickness is not unto death, but for the glory of God, that the Son of God might be glorified thereby.**

Lazarus was the brother **of Mary and her sister Martha.** We know something of the sisters from Luke 10:38-42. Martha was the active worker, and Mary was more contemplative. John identified Mary in verse 2 as the one who **anointed** Jesus at a meal given after Lazarus was raised from the dead (John 12:1-9). Nothing is said about any other family members, so apparently these were single siblings. We learn that **Lazarus was sick.** This doesn't make him unique because sickness is part of life in an imperfect world. The sisters loved their brother and felt that he was seriously ill. The most important fact about the three was that they were Jesus' friends. In their message to Jesus, they referred to Lazarus as **he whom thou lovest.** Verse 5 tells us "Jesus loved Martha, Mary, and Lazarus."

At the time of Martha's and Mary's message, Jesus was in Perea, a two-day journey from Bethany (10:40). The tone of the sisters' message to Jesus was urgent but not demanding. They did not insist that Jesus come immediately, though they perhaps expected that He would. They were very concerned about Lazarus. Their action reminds us that in similar situations we should tell our troubles to Jesus.

Verse 4 records Jesus' initial response to the message from the sisters. He said, **This sickness is not unto death** ("will not end in death," NIV). Jesus was not saying that Lazarus would not die from this sickness. The disciples seem to have understood Him to mean this. Later Jesus said, "Our friend Lazarus has fallen asleep, but I am going there to wake him up." They replied, "Lord, if he sleeps, he will get better." Jesus then said plainly, "Lazarus is dead" (vv. 11-14, NIV). The end result of Lazarus's sickness was to be **the glory of God, that the Son of God might be glorified thereby.**

Sickness and death are realities in our sinful world. They are part of the curse that sin brought into the world. Many people try to deny the reality of death, especially their own. Life contains many reminders of our mortality. The death of family and friends is one such reminder. The passing of time so quickly is another. Have you ever walked through an old cemetery and read the dates on the stones? That will give you perspective. Or have you traced your family tree? The number of generations and their swift exit from life reminds us that we all will die—if the Lord delays His coming. "It is appointed unto men once to die, but after this the judgment" (Heb. 9:27). This is one appointment we all will keep.

What are the lasting lessons of verses 1-4?

1. Sickness and death are realities of earthly life.

2. Especially when sickness comes or death threatens, we should take our needs to Jesus.

3. Although many people seek to deny their death, this is one appointment that we all will keep.

Believers Experience Resurrection and Life (John 11:21-27)

Were Martha's first words to Jesus a rebuke or an expression of faith? Does verse 22 indicate that Martha expected Jesus to raise Lazarus from the dead? What did Martha believe about resurrection? Why are verses 25-26 so powerful? What two promises do they contain? Was Martha's confession of faith adequate?

Verses 21-22: **Then said Martha unto Jesus, Lord, if thou hadst been here, my brother had not died. 22But I know, that even now, whatsoever thou wilt ask of God, God will give it thee.**

Verses 5-20 bridge the gap between verses 4 and 21. Jesus loved the three siblings, but He stayed two days before leaving for Bethany. Why did He not leave right away? One factor is that Jesus was two days away. When He arrived in Bethany, Lazarus had been dead four days. If the messengers took two days to reach Jesus, and Jesus took two days going from Perea to Bethany, Lazarus already would have died before He arrived.

Why then did He delay? He could have at least arrived sooner to help comfort the grieving sisters. The best answer may be to compare this incident with other times in John's Gospel when Jesus insisted on operating on His own time schedule (2:1-4; 7:1-10).

When Martha heard Jesus was coming, she went out to meet Him. She said, **Lord, if thou hadst been here, my brother had not died.** Was this an expression of faith or a rebuke of Jesus for delaying? Some people see verse 21 as a rebuke of Jesus for failing to come in time to heal Lazarus. However, Martha's words were not so much a rebuke as an expression of her grief at losing her brother and an expression of faith that Jesus could have healed Lazarus.

Verse 22 is a strong statement of Martha's faith in Jesus: **Even now, whatsoever thou wilt ask of God, God will give it thee.** What did she mean? Was she expecting Jesus to raise Lazarus from the dead? If so, why did she later object to Jesus' order to open the tomb (v. 39)? Hers was a struggle between the darkness of grief and the light of hope. Even though she may not have formed a strong belief about what Jesus would do, Martha's words show she was willing to leave the issue in Jesus' hands. She was confident God would enable Jesus to do whatever was needed.

Verses 23-27: **Jesus saith unto her, Thy brother shall rise again. 24Martha saith unto him, I know that he shall rise again in the resurrection at the last day. 25Jesus said unto her, I am the resurrection, and the life: he that believeth in me, though he were dead, yet shall**

he live: [26]and whosoever liveth and believeth in me shall never die. Believest thou this? [27]She saith unto him, Yea, Lord: I believe that thou art the Christ, the Son of God, which should come into the world.

Although the Sadducees did not believe in a future resurrection, the Pharisees and many of the common people did. Therefore, when Jesus told Martha, **thy brother shall rise again,** she assumed He was speaking of **the resurrection at the last day.** For her, resurrection was a future event of the end time. Jesus challenged her by saying, **I am the resurrection, and the life.** He did not deny the future resurrection as an event, but He claimed that the resurrection is a person, and He is that resurrection. She did not need to wait for a distant event; she needed to rely on His immediate presence.

Of all Jesus' "I am" statements, this one speaks most clearly to our human plight and claims the most for Jesus. He made two promises. The first one in verse 25 relates to His title as **the resurrection,** and the second one relates to His title as **the life.** William Hendriksen offered a good summary: "Jesus is *the resurrection;* hence, 'he who believes in me, *though he die, yet shall he live.*' Jesus is *the life;* hence, 'everyone *who lives* and believes in me *shall never, never die.*'"[1]

The words translated **though he were dead** are clearer when translated "though he may die" (NKJV), "even though he dies" (NIV), or "even if he dies" (HCSB). Jesus was acknowledging death's reality for everyone, including His followers; but He was promising that death is not the end. The One who is the Resurrection will deliver believers from and through death into life.

Notice three things about verses 25-26. (1) Jesus made two promises: victory over death and everlasting life beyond death. (2) This victory over death is not found through belief in a doctrine but in a personal relationship with Jesus Christ. (3) We experience eternal life when we come to know Jesus.

Jesus asked Martha if she believed Him—**Believest thou this?** Her answer is a confession of faith that reads much like Peter's confession of faith at Caesarea Philippi (Matt. 16:16). Also like Peter, the confession showed growing faith. Hers was the faith of a pilgrim who was still learning and growing. She affirmed her faith in Jesus as the Messiah of Israel **(the Christ).** She also believed that revelation had shown Jesus to be **the Son of God.** He also was the One who had been promised to **come into the world.** Some Bible students think that Martha missed the point of verses 25-26. I prefer to see her in the same perspective as the man born blind. She responded to divine light each time she received new light.

John 11:25-26 is a passage often read at funerals. For true believers, this is a precious promise; but too many lack the faith to claim Jesus' promise. The play *The Best Man* contains a poignant scene about facing death. Two politicians are discussing God, religion, and the hereafter. Both men admit that they believe neither in God nor in life after death. One man is an old veteran politician. He tells his younger colleague that he is dying of cancer; the doctor has given him a few months to live. The younger man is shocked and deeply concerned about his friend, but he cannot think of anything reassuring to say. Finally he tries by saying: "But there's hope in this: Every act we make sets off a chain of reaction which never ends. And if we are reasonably . . . good, well, there *is* some consolation in that, a kind of immortality." The old politician replied dryly, "I suggest you tell yourself that when *you* finally have to face a whole pile of nothin' up ahead."[2]

What are the lasting lessons in verses 21-27?

1. Believers can express honest feelings of grief and their questions to Jesus.
2. Jesus sometimes seems to delay answering our requests, but He operates on His schedule, not ours.
3. There will be a future resurrection, but Jesus is the Resurrection.
4. Eternal life begins when we meet Jesus.
5. Jesus asks us if we believe Him.

Jesus Is Sovereign over Death (John 11:38-40,43-44)

*What emotions did Jesus express as he approached Lazarus's tomb? Why did Martha object to opening the tomb? How does faith relate to **the glory of God**? Why was Lazarus's resurrection such a powerful sign of Jesus' power? How was Jesus' resurrection unique? How does Jesus exercise His sovereignty over death?*

Verse 38: **Jesus therefore again groaning in himself cometh to the grave. It was a cave, and a stone lay upon it.**

Verses 28-37 are important in understanding the rest of the verses. Martha went home and told Mary that Jesus was calling for her. She immediately went to Him and was followed by the mourners. Mary said the same thing Martha said in verse 21. Then she joined the mourners in loud weeping. When Jesus saw them weeping, "he groaned in the spirit, and was troubled" (v. 33). When Jesus asked where Lazarus was buried, they told Him to come and see. "Jesus wept" (v. 35). The mourners took this as a sign of Jesus' love for Lazarus, and they asked if the One who healed the man born blind could not have healed Lazarus.

The word **groaning** in verse 38 is the same word in verse 33. The Greek word originally referred to the snorting of a horse. It came to mean "to be angry." Some Bible students insist that this is the meaning here. In fact, this is the way the *Holman Christian Standard Bible* renders it in both verses: "He was angry in His spirit and deeply moved" (v. 33) and "Then Jesus, angry in Himself again, came to the tomb" (v. 38). Other Bible students and translations soften the meaning by using more neutral words: "He was deeply moved in spirit and troubled" (v. 33, NIV) and "Jesus, once more deeply moved, came to the tomb" (v. 38, NIV). Jesus obviously had strong feelings. What caused His anger or His deep emotion? Some feel that Jesus was angry, or at least greatly upset, by the unbelief of the mourners. Some even include Martha and Mary among those with whom Jesus was upset. Others believe that Jesus was upset by the deep grief of humanity in the face of death or that He was upset about sin and death that plague people.

One key question is how Jesus' **groaning in himself** relates to the words "Jesus wept." The verb for "wept" in verse 35 appears only here in the New Testament. It is a different word from the "weeping" of the people in verse 33. The most natural way to understand Jesus' tears is that He entered into the grief felt by the sisters and by all who are bereaved. He was going to raise Lazarus to life, yet He was touched by their grief. Without doubt we can see this as a sign that the Lord is sympathetic with those who lose loved ones.

Verses 39-40,43-44: **Jesus said, Take ye away the stone. Martha, the sister of him that was dead, saith unto him, Lord, by this time he stinketh: for he hath been dead four days. 40Jesus saith unto her, Said I not unto thee, that, if thou wouldest believe, thou shouldest see the glory of God?**

. . . .

43And when he thus had spoken, he cried with a loud voice, Lazarus, come forth. 44And he that was dead came forth, bound hand and foot with graveclothes: and his face was bound about with a napkin. Jesus saith unto them, Loose him, and let him go.

When Jesus ordered that **the stone** be taken **away, Martha** objected. Some see this as evidence of her unbelief. She obviously had not expected this. Martha seems to have been the older of the two sisters. She apparently had to agree to allow the tomb to be opened. The fact that she initially objected was out of her sense of respect for her brother. In fact, she gave as her reason for objecting the fact that Lazarus had **been dead four days** and his decomposing body would have "a bad odor" (NIV). The Jews believed the soul lingered near the body for three days; thus a person who had been dead four days was hopelessly dead. Decay was beginning. This is why the Bible emphasizes that Lazarus had been dead four days.

Martha heard Jesus' challenge that those who believe **see the glory of God. Glory** refers to the majesty of God, seeing God for who He is. These words apparently caused Martha to allow the tomb to be opened. Jesus then **cried with a loud voice, Lazarus, come forth.** Imagine the reaction of the mourners when Lazarus emerged with the wrappings still on his body! Jesus did what only God could do.

During His earthly ministry, Jesus raised at least three people from death back to life: the widow of Nain's only son (Luke 7:11-17), Jairus's daughter (8:49-56), and Lazarus. Two important facts need to be noted. For one thing, each of these foreshadowed the resurrection of Jesus Christ from the dead. Second, these three people were restored to physical life, but being mortal, they died again later. By contrast, Jesus died once never again to die. He conquered death. He rose from the dead. He has dominion over death (Rom. 6:9). He is alive forever, and He has the keys to death and the grave (Rev. 1:18).

Throughout history, many people have hoped for a life after death. There have been various ideas about the nature of this life and many different beliefs about how to have life after death. Some of these hopes are based on human feelings. People stand and look at the body of a dead loved one and cannot believe the person is not still alive somewhere. Or they realize that people only begin to make a contribution to life when death takes them. There must be some way that the person can continue, they feel. The New Testament bases the confidence of eternal life squarely on the fact that God raised Jesus His Son from the dead. "Praise be to the God and Father of our Lord Jesus Christ! In his great mercy he has given us new birth into a living hope through the resurrection of Jesus Christ from the dead" (1 Pet. 1:3, NIV). "O death, where is thy sting? O grave, where is thy victory? The sting of death is sin; and the strength of sin is the law. But thanks be to God, which giveth us the victory through our Lord Jesus Christ" (1 Cor. 15:55-57).

Biblical hope is a resurrection hope. This is different from the hopes of some of the Greeks and of various religions today that view the body as evil and see death as a friend that sets the soul free from the prison of the body. Often this kind of thinking includes belief in the pre-existence of souls and reincarnation of souls at death from one body to another. The biblical view is that although sin corrupts the body, the body will be resurrected. This is possible only by the power of the Lord. Death is not a friend but an enemy. Christ defeated death. Thus death is an enemy now under the dominion of the Lord.

Through His resurrection from the dead, Jesus Christ won the victory over sin and death. The door to the kingdom of heaven is open for all to enter. Through faith in the One who is the Resurrection and the Life, you can know that you have entered eternal life.

❖ *Spiritual Transformations*

Sickness and death are realities. Jesus is the Resurrection who will lead you in life and through death into eternity. He is the Life that begins with faith and never ends. Jesus raised Lazarus from the dead, thus foreshadowing His own resurrection. By these two acts He showed His sovereignty over death.

Many people try to deny death by living as if they never will die. This is foolish because death is certain unless Christ returns first. Either way, wise people prepare for the certainty of death. Jesus Himself is our hope in life, in sickness, in bereavement, and in death. Faith in Him is essential for Him to help us in life and in death. People have wistful hopes of life after death, but Jesus, who is the Resurrection and the Life, is the only sure basis for hope.

On what or on whom are you basing your hope of life after death?

____

How does faith in the risen Lord affect how you live and think? ___

____

Prayer of Commitment: Lord, I praise You for Your victory over death and for giving eternal life to me. Amen.

[1]William Hendriksen, *Exposition of the Gospel of John*, vol. 2 [Grand Rapids: Baker Book House, 1954], 150.

[2]Gore Vidal, *The Best Man* [Boston: Little, Brown and Company, 1960], 41-42.

Week of April 27

THE BREAD OF LIFE

Background Passage: John 6:1-59
Focal Passage: John 6:5-13,24-27,32-35
Key Verse: John 6:35

❖ *Significance of the Lesson*

- The *Theme* of the lesson is that Jesus provides for His followers.
- The *Life Question* this lesson seeks to address is, How does Jesus provide for my needs?
- The *Biblical Truth* is that Jesus is able and willing to provide all that people need in life.
- The *Life Impact* is to help you trust Jesus daily to provide for your needs.

Jesus and Our Needs

The prevailing secular mind-set sees no connection between faith in Jesus and the provision of life's needs. For one thing, secular people often fail to distinguish between wants and needs. People err in one of two directions. (1) They define *wants* as *needs,* and then they lose faith when Jesus fails to give them all they want. (2) They think they meet their own needs.

The biblical worldview trusts Jesus to supply whatever we need to do His will. He is able and willing to meet our physical and spiritual needs. Faith in Him means trusting Him to decide what we need and to supply that in His own way. Our deepest needs are always moral and spiritual.

Word Study: *bread from heaven* and *bread of God*

Pious Jews refused to use God's personal name. They used various words to signify God. One of these words was *heaven.* Thus "bread from heaven" refers to the same reality as "bread of God."

Bread brought to the Jews' minds the manna God sent to feed their forefathers in the wilderness. Jesus tried to get them to see that He was the true Bread of life, of which the manna and even their daily bread were only signs.

❖ *Search the Scriptures*

Jesus saw the need of the crowd for bread—physical and spiritual. The disciples saw no way they could feed so many people. Jesus turned the five loaves and two small fish into more than enough to feed thousands. When the crowd followed Jesus the next day, He told them they were only interested in physical bread. He told them He wanted to give them eternal life.

How does Jesus provide for your needs? The Focal Passage Outline gives four answers to this Life Question.

Jesus Knows What Is Needed (John 6:5-9)

What was the background and setting of this event? What question did Jesus ask Philip? What information did Andrew share? What do we know about the boy? What needs was Jesus seeking to meet?

Verses 5-9: **When Jesus then lifted up his eyes, and saw a great company come unto him, he saith unto Philip, Whence shall we buy bread, that these may eat? 6And this he said to prove him: for he himself knew what he would do. 7Philip answered him, Two hundred pennyworth of bread is not sufficient for them, that everyone of them may take a little. 8One of his disciples, Andrew, Simon Peter's brother, saith unto him, 9There is a lad here, which hath five barley loaves, and two small fishes: but what are they among so many?**

Feeding the 5,000 is the only miracle of Jesus' ministry that is found in all four Gospels. All tell of the same miracle, but each includes some distinctive details. John's account is the most distinctive. Only John mentions Philip, Andrew, and the boy. Only John tells of the attempt of the people to make Jesus a king, and only he tells of the confrontation of Jesus with the people on the day following the miracle when Jesus gave the bread of life discourse. All of John 6 has to do directly or indirectly with the miracle.

When we look at all four Gospels, we learn about the background and setting for the miracle. Jesus was at the height of His popularity in Galilee. In fact, so many people were coming for healing that He and the disciples found no time even to eat (Mark 6:31). Jesus and the disciples sought to withdraw from the crowds by crossing the Sea of Galilee to the eastern side (Matt. 14:13; Mark 6:31-32; John 6:1). However, the people discovered where He had gone and followed Him there (Matt. 14:13; Mark 6:33; Luke 9:11; John 6:2). **Jesus then lifted up his eyes, and saw a great company come unto him.** Instead of seeing this as an interruption or intrusion, Jesus had compassion on the multitude (Matt. 14:14; Mark 6:34). Jesus welcomed them and spoke to them of the kingdom of God (Luke 9:11). He also healed those who needed to be healed (Matt. 14:14; Luke 9:11).

As evening approached, the disciples realized that these people soon would need to eat. They suggested that the people be sent into nearby towns to seek food (Matt. 14:15; Mark 6:35-36; Luke 9:12). Jesus told the disciples to feed the people, but they protested that they did not have enough money to feed so many, adding that they had only five loaves and two fish (Matt. 14:16-17; Mark 6:37-38; Luke 9:13). John's Gospel focuses on Jesus' words to one disciple, **Philip.** Jesus asked him, **Whence** ("where," NIV) **shall we buy bread, that these may eat?** John tells us that Jesus asked Philip this question in order **to prove him. Prove** is *peirazon,* which can mean either "tempt" or "test." Jesus does not tempt; therefore, the meaning here is "test" (NIV). We are not told why Jesus felt the need to test Philip's faith.

Perhaps Philip was good with numbers and money, or perhaps he had had experience buying food to feed large numbers. At any rate, Philip already had made a rough calculation of the cost of feeding so many people. He calculated that **two hundred pennyworth** ("denarii," NASB, HCSB) **of bread** would not be enough for each person to have even **a little. Pennyworth** translates *denarion.* A *denarius* was a Roman coin. Based on the pay scale in Matthew 20:1-16, we know that one of these coins was paid to workers for a day's work. Thus 200 of these would be what a day laborer could earn in that many days. This was no fortune, but it was a considerable sum. Jesus and the twelve kept a moneybag to help the poor (John 12:6), but they did not have this much money. In this passage, Philip is like people who refuse to seek to meet some great need because they say, "We can't afford it." If the need is one the Lord is seeking to meet, He is willing and able to provide what is needed to do it.

Jesus **knew what he would do,** but Philip and the others seem not to have trusted Jesus to meet such needs of so many. **Andrew** spoke up at this point. He is identified as **Simon Peter's brother,** reminding readers that Andrew was the one who told Simon that Jesus was the Messiah (1:40-42). Andrew is mentioned in only three accounts in John's Gospel, and each time he was bringing someone to Jesus. Here he brought the **lad** with the **loaves** and **fishes.** Later, when some Greeks came to see Jesus, Philip informed Andrew, who told Jesus (12:20-22).

Lad translates *paidarion,* which refers to a young boy. Storytellers and preachers have used their imaginations to explain the boy, his food, how Andrew discovered the boy and his lunch, and why the boy allowed Jesus to have his food. Verses 8-9 tells us all we know for sure. Surely the boy offered to share his food; Andrew would not have taken the boy's food without his permission. So to his credit, the child was willing to give all he had to Jesus. We can congratulate Andrew on his telling Jesus of the available food; but like Philip, he failed to recognize what Jesus was able to do.

Five barley loaves were made of the cheapest kind of grain, and they were not what we call *loaves.* They were more like pancakes. The **two small fishes** were something like sardines in size. This is what Jesus had available to meet the needs of thousands of hungry people. To the disciples, the resources available seemed totally inadequate to meet the needs of so many. As Andrew asked, **What are they among so many?**

What are the lasting lessons in verses 5-9?

1. Jesus sees interruptions as opportunities.
2. Jesus is moved with compassion on people.
3. Jesus knows and cares about human needs of all kinds.
4. Followers of Jesus sometimes feel that their limited resources are not sufficient to meet what seem to be overwhelming needs.

Jesus Multiplies What Is Available (John 6:10-13)

How did Jesus organize for meeting needs? What example did He set by thanking God for what He had? How did He use that little to feed so many? What did Jesus teach about not wasting?

Verses 10-13: **And Jesus said, Make the men sit down. Now there was much grass in the place. So the men sat down, in number about**

five thousand. 11And Jesus took the loaves; and when he had given
thanks, he distributed to the disciples, and the disciples to them
that were set down; and likewise of the fishes as much as they
would. 12When they were filled, he said unto his disciples, Gather
up the fragments that remain, that nothing be lost. 13Therefore
they gathered them together, and filled twelve baskets with the
fragments of the five barley loaves, which remained over and above
unto them that had eaten.

Jesus organized the people and the disciples. He told the disciples to have the people to **sit down** on the **grass.** The people were seated in groups of hundreds and fifties (Mark 6:40). Jesus used the twelve to distribute the food. Organization is not an evil if it achieves the Lord's purpose.

However, Jesus did not distribute the food until **he had given thanks.** He had only five loaves and two small fish, but He thanked God for what He had. Jesus thus set the example in thanking God for food. God is the giver of food and all things good. We should thank Him, not take credit for ourselves. We also should pray, "Give us this day our daily bread" (Matt. 6:11) since we are dependent on God for all our needs.

Then Jesus **distributed** food **to the disciples,** who distributed it to the people. They gave to each one as much bread and fish **as they would** ("wanted," NIV). Thus all were filled up. Verse 10 in the *King James Version* has **men** twice. However, the first use of the word translates *anthropous,* which refers to "people" (NIV, HCSB). The second use of the word translates *andres,* which refers to adult males. Since there were about five thousand men, the total number including women and children was several thousand more.

Jesus ordered the disciples to collect what was left, and they **filled twelve baskets with the fragments of the five barley loaves.** This further showed the magnitude of the miracle. It also showed that Jesus believed food should not be wasted. This is a lesson needed in our "throw away" society.

How did five loaves and two fish feed so many? The Bible obviously considered this a miracle performed by Jesus. Some people try to rationalize what happened. Some claim that many people had brought lunches but had not shown them until the boy shared his. Then, according to this view, the miracle was that the people shared with one another. This idea misses the point of the Bible miracle.

This miracle was one of the miraculous signs of Jesus. It was a miracle with a message. What was the message? One message was that Jesus is able to take little and multiply it to meet vast human needs.

What are the lasting lessons of verses 10-13?

1. We should thank God for food and His other provisions.
2. We should recognize our dependence on God.
3. Jesus is willing and able to meet human needs.
4. He can multiply our little to accomplish much.

Jesus Reveals What Is Important (John 6:24-27)

What happened between verse 13 and verse 24? Why did the crowds follow Jesus around the sea? What accusation did Jesus make against them? How is the word ***saw*** *used in verse 26? What title did Jesus use for Himself? What is the significance of the word* ***give*** *in verse 27?*

Verses 24-27: **When the people therefore saw that Jesus was not there, neither his disciples, they also took shipping, and came to Capernaum, seeking for Jesus. [25]And when they had found him on the other side of the sea, they said unto him, Rabbi, when camest thou hither? [26]Jesus answered them and said, Verily, verily, I say unto you, Ye seek me, not because ye saw the miracles, but because ye did eat of the loaves, and were filled. [27]Labor not for the meat which perisheth, but for that meat which endureth unto everlasting life, which the Son of man shall give unto you: for him hath God the Father sealed.**

Verse 24 sums up considerable action between the miraculous sign on one day and the confrontation with Jesus on the next day (v. 22). Verses 14-15 are keys to understanding the confrontation. Immediately after Jesus fed the 5,000, the people acclaimed Jesus as "that prophet that should come into the world." When they tried to "take him by force, to make him a king, he departed again into a mountain himself alone." Mark 6:45 tells us that Jesus had "constrained his disciples to get into the ship, and to go to the other side." This implies that the disciples were sympathetic with this move to make Jesus into their kind of king.

When the people got up the next day, they looked for Jesus until they realized that He had gone to the other side of the lake (vv. 22-23). Then they **took shipping, and came to Capernaum,**

seeking for Jesus. When they had found him, they asked, **Rabbi, when camest thou hither? Rabbi** was their word for "teacher." This was a respected position, but it was far short of prophet, king, Messiah, or Son of God.

Jesus ignored their greeting and question. He went to the heart of the issue by accusing them of seeking Him **not because** they **saw the miracles, but because** they **did eat of the loaves, and were filled.** They had seen the miracle with their own eyes, but they had not recognized the meaning of the miracle. **Miracle** translates *semeia,* "miraculous sign" (NIV). This word refers to the meaning of the miracle. The people totally missed Jesus' purpose in feeding them. He did it not just because they were hungry. He did it to signify by the bread their deeper spiritual needs.

Many people see only their physical needs. They fail to recognize their spiritual needs. Jesus is concerned for all our needs, but His greatest concern is for our spiritual needs. We need to minister in His name to all human needs, but our ultimate goal is to win people to saving faith in Christ. Christian ministries include feeding the hungry, healing the sick, housing the homeless, and so on. This is true on the mission fields as it is at home. Medical personnel, builders, and relief workers meet human needs in the name of the Lord, but their ultimate objective is to lead people to find eternal life in Christ.

Verse 27 is crucial in this lesson. The first part of the verse contains a warning against working **for the meat which perisheth. Meat** translates *brosin,* which means "food" (NIV), not just meat. This is a twofold warning. For one thing, it warns against focusing attention on material things as our greatest needs. Jesus elsewhere said, "Take heed, and beware of covetousness: for a man's life consisteth not in the abundance of the things which he possesseth" (Luke 12:15). He went on to tell the parable of the rich fool to illustrate this important truth (vv. 16-21). The second part of the warning is not to spend your time and energy working for only material things. He said, "Lay not up for yourselves treasures upon earth, where moth and rust doth corrupt, and where thieves break through and steal: but lay up for yourselves treasures in heaven, where neither moth nor rust doth corrupt, and where thieves do not break through nor steal: for where your treasure is, there will your heart be also" (Matt. 6:19-21).

The last part of verse 27 stresses that the life that Jesus offers is not something we work for and earn. It is something that **the Son of**

man shall give unto us. Notice the word **give.** Only **the Son of man** can **give** us **everlasting life.**

Jesus fed the crowd because of their hunger, but He wanted them to see their deeper need for the life that only God can give. Unfortunately, many of those who ate the bread and fish failed to see what Jesus wanted them to see. We need food to live on this earth. But we need the Bread of life to live in God's eternal kingdom.

What are the lasting lessons in verses 24-27?

1. People often are concerned only about their physical needs.
2. Some people are willing to follow Jesus if He promises to meet their physical needs.
3. Jesus met physical needs as signs of His desire to meet spiritual needs.
4. We cannot meet our own deepest needs by our own efforts. Jesus gives everlasting life to those who trust in Him.

Jesus Provides What Is Lasting (John 6:32-35)

What misconceptions about manna did Jesus correct? What parallels are there between these verses and Jesus' interview with the woman at the well in John 4? Why is faith a crucial issue? How is this ***I am*** *statement similar to the others?*

Verses 32-35: **Then Jesus said unto them, Verily, verily, I say unto you, Moses gave you not that bread from heaven; but my Father giveth you the true bread from heaven. 33For the bread of God is he which cometh down from heaven, and giveth life unto the world. 34Then said they unto him, Lord, evermore give us this bread. 35And Jesus said unto them, I am the bread of life: he that cometh to me shall never hunger; and he that believeth on me shall never thirst.**

When Jesus spoke of **bread from heaven,** the people naturally thought of the manna that their forefathers had eaten in the wilderness. Jesus corrected two misunderstandings about the manna. They emphasized Moses' role in providing the manna. Jesus stressed that God, not Moses, had given them the manna. Many Jews of Jesus' day expected the messiah to restore the giving of manna. Jesus insisted that what God was giving them was not manna like that in the wilderness but the One who is Himself **the bread of life.** Jesus is **the true bread from heaven.** Notice the word **true.** The word **bread** is another example of a word being used one way by the people and another way by Jesus. When Jesus spoke to Nicodemus of a new birth, Nicodemus assumed at first that Jesus was speaking of physical birth, but Jesus showed that He meant new birth in the Spirit (3:1-8). When Jesus spoke to the woman of Samaria, she assumed that He was talking about water like that she had drawn from the well. When He told her that whoever drank of the water He would give would never be thirsty, the woman said, "Give me this water, that I thirst not, neither come hither to draw" (4:15). In the same way, when Jesus told the crowd that He came to bring them **bread from heaven,** they said, **Lord, evermore give us this bread.** But they were thinking not of Jesus as the Bread but of bread they could eat as their forefathers ate manna in the wilderness. That's when Jesus said, **I am the bread of life: he that cometh to me shall never hunger; and he that believeth on me shall never thirst.** This is similar to what He told the woman at the well: "Whosoever drinketh of this water shall thirst again: but whosoever drinketh of the water that I shall give him shall never thirst; but the water that I shall give him shall be in him a well of water springing up into everlasting life" (4:13-14).

Notice several things. First of all, Jesus Himself is the water and the bread. As we noted at the beginning of this study, Christianity is not primarily a way of life, a set of beliefs, or a mystical experience; it is a person—Jesus Christ. Second, the water and the bread signify the life that Jesus offers. Jesus is the giver of physical and spiritual life. Third, the life Jesus gives is real, abundant, and eternal. Life in Christ begins with the new birth and never ends. Fourth, only those who believe in Jesus receive the life He offers to all. By the same token, those who reject Him miss the life He offers.

Malcolm Muggeridge was a British magazine editor and writer. During most of his life he was known for his sharp and sometimes stinging wit. Late in life he was converted and turned his writing skill over to the Lord. Here is how he described in picturesque language His experience with Christ: "I grasped that over it lay, as it were, a cable-bridge, frail, swaying, but passable. And this bridge, this reconciliation between the black despair of lying bound and gagged in the tiny dungeon of ego, and soaring upwards into the white radiance of God's universal love—this bridge was the Incarnation, whose truth expresses that of the desperate need it meets. Because of our physical hunger we know there is bread; because of our spiritual hunger we know there is Christ."[1]

What are the lasting lessons of verses 32-35?

1. Some people are willing to follow Jesus if He meets their expectations of providing for their physical needs.

2. Jesus met physical needs such as hunger and thirst to signify the spiritual and eternal needs that only He can meet.

3. Real faith in Jesus is necessary to receive the life Jesus offers.

❖ *Spiritual Transformations*

When the multitudes needed food, the disciples lacked faith that they could provide it. Jesus miraculously fed the multitude with only five loaves and two small fish. When the people kept following Jesus, He accused them of seeking Him only for the food He provided. He said that the bread signified that He is the Bread of life, who would satisfy their spiritual needs forever.

How does Jesus provide for your needs? The four answers given in this lesson are these: He knows our needs and is willing and able to meet them. He can multiply our limited resources to meet our needs and the needs of others. He came to meet the deepest human needs, which are spiritual. Only through faith in Him as Lord can He give us life that is real, abundant, and eternal.

Do you trust Jesus to meet your needs? ____________________

How do you seek to meet overwhelming needs with limited resources? ____________________

____

Prayer of Commitment: Lord, help me to look to You to provide for all my needs, not merely for my physical needs but for my true needs. Sustain me and nourish me as only You can do. Amen.

[1]Malcolm Muggeridge, "Bread and Spiritual Hunger," in *The Book of Jesus*, edited by Calvin Miller [New York: Simon & Schuster, 1996], 236.

Study Theme

Family Members Showing Grace

Because this is the Family Bible Study Series, we often look at Bible teachings about families. Because May is the traditional time for a family emphasis, this is often the time for such studies. This month has a four-session study on "Family Members Showing Grace."

"Establishing Godly Standards for My Family" is based on the story of the Rechabites [REK-uh-bights] in Jeremiah 35. This is not one of the more familiar family Bible passages, but it has a powerful message of the effect of one man's commitment on succeeding generations of his family. Jonadab [JAHN-uh-dab] made a commitment not to live in houses, plant vineyards, or drink wine. Centuries later his descendants kept his way of life.

"Making Peace in My Family" is based on the more familiar account of Abraham and his nephew Lot. Abraham headed off conflict by offering Lot the choice of land. Abraham, as the elder, could have made the choice, but he gave this right to his nephew.

"Giving Unselfishly to God's Work" is based on the contrasting actions of Barnabas and of Ananias and Sapphira in giving to meet the needs of the poor in the Jerusalem church. Barnabas was generous; the married couple lied to the Holy Spirit.

"Serving God Together as a Family" is based on the biblical references to that remarkable married couple, Aquila and Priscilla. They always acted as a team in helping Paul, in helping Apollos, in risking their lives for Paul, and in having churches meet in their houses.

This study considers how grace impacts family life and behavior. Lessons explore how God's grace transforms families by changing their attitudes and actions. This Study Theme is designed to help you

- establish and model godly, enduring standards for your family (May 4)
- work for peace in your family (May 11)
- develop a lifestyle of giving unselfishly to God's work (May 18)
- regularly serve God with family members (May 25)

Week of May 4

ESTABLISHING GODLY STANDARDS FOR MY FAMILY

Background Passage: Jeremiah 35:1-19
Focal Passage: Jeremiah 35:1-2,5-10,12-19
Key Verses: Jeremiah 35:18-19

❖ *Significance of the Lesson*

• The *Theme* of the lesson is that families can be different from the world by obeying God.

• The *Life Question* this lesson seeks to address is, How can I help my family establish godly standards?

• The *Biblical Truth* is that God expects His people to follow His standards.

• The *Life Impact* is to help you establish and model godly, enduring standards for your family.

Family Standards

In a secular worldview, families generally choose to blend with society around them. They follow worldly standards and set worldly goals. In the biblical worldview, God commands individuals and families to be different from the world. He expects them to obey Him rather than giving in to cultural moral attitudes and values.

Who Were the Rechabites?

A Kenite named Hemath is called "the father of the house of Rechab" (1 Chron. 2:55). One of the Rechabites [REK-uh-bights] was named Jehonadab [jih-HAHN-uh-dab] (Jonadab [JAHN-uh-dab]). He was active in supporting Jehu in destroying the dynasty of Ahab in Northern Israel and in killing the priests of Baal (2 Kings 10:15,25). He also taught his family not to drink wine, build houses, or plant vineyards. About 250 years later, the descendants of Jonadab remained loyal to their ancestor's teachings.

Word Study: *instruction*

The word rendered **instruction** in Jeremiah 35:13 is the Hebrew word *musar*. This word is derived from *yasar*, which means "to discipline," "to correct," or "to chasten." Thus the noun in verse 13 refers to the kind of instruction that is designed to correct, discipline, or chasten. The word *musar* is found most often in the Book of Proverbs, which was written to instruct young men in how to live.

❖ *Search the Scriptures*

God told Jeremiah to offer the Rechabites wine to drink. They refused because of their family heritage going back to Jonadab, who forbade drinking wine, living in houses, or planting vineyards. God then told the people of Judah that the Rechabites had obeyed the words of their ancestor, but that the people of Judah refused to obey the word of the Lord. God promised the Rechabites a blessing for their faithfulness.

The three points of the Focal Passage Outline are ways to achieve the Life Impact of establishing and modeling enduring godly standards for your family.

Model an Obedient Lifestyle (Jer. 35:1-2,5-10)

When did these events take place? Why did God tell Jeremiah to offer wine to a group of abstainers? Why did they refuse to drink the wine? What can one person achieve? How does each family teach moral values?

Verses 1-2,5: **The word which came unto Jeremiah from the LORD in the days of Jehoiakim the son of Josiah king of Judah, saying,**
2Go unto the house of the Rechabites, and speak unto them, and bring them into the house of the LORD, into one of the chambers, and give them wine to drink.

. . . .

5And I set before the sons of the house of the Rechabites pots full of wine, and cups, and I said unto them, Drink ye wine.

Throughout the Book of Jeremiah, we find such words as these: **the word which came unto Jeremiah from the LORD.** Jeremiah was speaking not for himself but for the Lord. This word came to the prophet **in the days of Jehoiakim** [jih-HOY-uh-kim] **the son of Josiah king of Judah.** Jeremiah began his ministry toward the end of the reign of the last good king of Judah, Josiah. Jeremiah's ministry continued under the reigns of the last kings of Judah, of whom Jehoiakim was one of the worst. Those were difficult times for the true people of God.

The Lord's command to Jeremiah must have sounded strange to him: **Go unto the house of the Rechabites** ("Recabites," NIV). **House** does not refer to their dwelling, for they had no houses. **House** means "family" (NIV). Jeremiah was told to **bring them into the house of the LORD, into one of the chambers.** The surprising words in verse 2 were God's order to **give them wine to drink.** The Rechabites were probably a large enough group that most people knew of them and their vow not to drink wine. Thus for Jeremiah to offer them wine and tell them to drink it would be like a preacher telling abstaining church members to drink wine. Can you imagine it?

Verses 3-4 show how Jeremiah carried out God's command. After bringing the Rechabites to a room in the temple, he **set before** them **pots full of wine, and cups.** Jeremiah left no doubt what they were being asked to do. **Drink ye wine,** he commanded. Jeremiah did this because he was told to do so by God. Why did God set up this situation? God doesn't tempt anyone, but He does test the faith and faithfulness of His people. And He does use His faithful people as object lessons for others' learning. Verses 12-17 show God used the Rechabites' obedience to challenge those who were disobedient.

Verses 6-10: **But they said, We will drink no wine: for Jonadab the son of Rechab our father commanded us, saying, Ye shall drink no wine, neither ye, nor your sons forever: 7neither shall ye build house, nor sow seed, nor plant vineyard, nor have any: but all your days ye shall dwell in tents; that ye may live many days in the land where ye be strangers. 8Thus have we obeyed the voice of Jonadab the son of Rechab our father in all that he hath charged us, to drink no wine all our days, we, our wives, our sons, nor our daughters; 9nor to build houses for us to dwell in: neither have we vineyard, nor field, nor seed: 10but we have dwelt in tents, and have obeyed, and done according to all that Jonadab our father commanded us.**

The Rechabites replied, **We will drink no wine.** They had moral convictions to which they remained true. Many people lack moral convictions. They have a flexible approach to life, in which they decide on issues of right and wrong when an issue comes up. What was the source of the Rechabites' convictions? Their source was a family heritage going back to **Jonadab. Jonadab** is called **the son of Rechab our father** ("our forefather Jonadab son of Recab," NIV). Jonadab was not literally the father of that generation. Nor was Jonadab literally the son of Rechab. In the Bible *father* often means "forefather" or "ancestor" and *son* often means "descendant." The family ancestor Jonadab lived over two centuries before the time of these events in Jeremiah 35.

What can one person do? Here was a man whose influence touched not only his immediate family but continued among his descendants not only for generations but also for centuries. One person's influence for God and good can be powerful. Jonadab's influence was on his descendants, and it was respected and followed for generations.

Jonadab made some personal decisions based on his understanding of what God wanted him to do—and he taught his children to live this way. Each succeeding set of parents passed this teaching and lifestyle on. Jonadab taught them, **Ye shall drink no wine, neither ye, nor your sons forever.** He also taught them not to **build house, nor sow seed, nor plant vineyard.** Instead, they were told to **dwell in tents.** By living this nomadic life, they could **live many days in the land where** they were **strangers.**

Why did Jonadab come to these convictions and why did he teach them to his family? Apparently he wanted his family to avoid the temptations of the people of the land. When the Israelites entered Canaan, God warned them against compromising their distinctive faith and way of life. They were to worship the one true God, and they were to be holy as He is holy. They were told to drive out or destroy the Baal worshipers of Canaan. By the time of Jonadab, he could see that the people had ignored this warning. The Israelites had become so slack that the king of Israel married a pagan princess, who proceeded to replace the worship of the Lord with the immoral and idolatrous worship of Baal. Jonadab concluded that he needed to get his family away from these evil influences, insofar as he could. The cities and towns were places where much evil was found. Wine often was part of the pagan lifestyle. Therefore, Jonadab chose to live a nomadic life in tents rather than build a house, plant a vineyard, and drink the wine.

Believers in every generation must struggle with the issue of how to relate to a culture that does not reflect the Lord's ways. Believers have tried three basic approaches. (1) Embrace the culture. (2) Avoid the culture. (3) Be in the culture but not of it.

We reject the first option as wrong. Unfortunately, in each generation many professed believers compromise their faith and way of life by following the sinful standards of the world. They are in the world, and they are of the world. No difference exists between how they live and how unbelievers live.

Throughout history some believers have sought to live apart from the places and people through whom they could be tempted. People go to places of retreat and prayer, where each person is committed to the same holy life. People move their residence from a place where sin is all around to a more sheltered environment. This is what Jonadab sought to do. He lived in tents with his family—away from the houses in settlements or cities where temptations were all around.

The third approach is to engage and interact with the culture—to be in but not of the world. When Jesus prayed for His disciples, He did not ask that they be taken out of the world, but that they be *in the world* without being *of the world* (John 17:14-16). Jesus befriended people of all kinds in order to witness to them. He was with sinners of all kinds, but He did not commit their sins. Throughout the Bible is this tension between the demand for personal holiness and the call to show God to all people.

Believers make moral and spiritual commitments according to which they seek to live. There are some places they won't go and some things they will not do. They abstain from intoxication through alcoholic beverages and illicit drugs. They refuse to open their minds to the filth of some books, magazines, movies, and television programs. They refuse to get caught up in blatant materialism. They do not seek anything first except the kingdom of God.

Many of us believe that we should totally abstain from beverage alcohol. Although drinking wine was practiced in biblical times, drunkenness was condemned (Prov. 20:1; 23:20,29-35). Drunkenness was associated with other sins of an ungodly life (Rom. 13:11-14; 1 Cor. 6:9-11). Alcohol slows down reflexes, leading to many deaths and injuries. It lowers moral inhibitions; thus it is often a factor in crime and sexual sins. Two other biblical principles provide a biblical basis for abstaining from beverage alcohol. For one thing, as Christians, we are to be good stewards of our bodies and our health (1 Cor. 6:19-20). Many drinkers become problem drinkers, and some become alcoholics. Only total abstainers avoid any possibility of these dangers to health and well being. Yet even if I knew I would never have such problems, another biblical principle deters me from drinking, even in moderation. That is the principle of influence on others (Rom. 14:21). If I drink, this will set the wrong example for my children and grandchildren. And it may negatively influence those who have a problem with alcohol.

Every family teaches ethics to family members. The ethics may be good or bad, but children are taught in the home how to live. Parents teach by what they say and by what they do. As someone said, "More is caught than taught." Both instruction and example are important. Jonadab practiced what he preached. Chester Swor, a Southern Baptist leader of a former generation, often stayed in private homes. He told of the contrast between two fathers. Both men were layman of wide usefulness in the church and community. They had good reputations. When Swor visited both homes, however, he met two very different men. One was the same at home as he was in public. He was a good example of Christian love and faith for his children. The other man was also thought well of in the community, but after visiting in his home, Swor wrote: "He gave vent to a long tirade of bitter criticism of a wide range of people, revealing that he was possessed of jealousy, arrogance, and pride. It was evident to me that there were real tensions between him and his family because of his domineering and thoughtless manner."[1]

No one knows you better than the people who live in the same house with you. Our families see us as we truly are. Blessed are those families who have a godly heritage that they cherish and pass on to others. We have looked at this Bible story from Jonadab's point of view. Look at it now from the point of view of his son. He had to make two choices. First, he had to decide to make his father's faith his own. Faith is not transmitted by heredity. Each must choose for himself. If the son chose (as he did in this case) to claim this heritage, he had to find ways to pass it along to his son. And so it was through each generation. Some people have a heritage of faith and love, but they choose to forsake it and to go their own ways. Others prize their heritage, claim it, and pass it on to their descendants.

What are the lasting lessons of verses 1-2,5-10?

1. Every family teaches how to live—either good or bad.
2. Children are influenced by how they are raised.
3. People can either claim or reject the moral example of their family.
4. Parents teach by what they say and by what they do.

5. One person can make a difference—even for generations to come.

6. Godly people seek to avoid evil people and evil situations.

Listen to the Lord (Jer. 35:12-17)

In what way was offering wine to the Rechabites a prophetic act? How well do we learn the lessons God seeks to teach us? How was the obedience of the Rechabites necessary for God to use them as an example? How did their obedience contrast with the actions of the people of Judah? How did God show His persistent love for the people of Judah? What was the punishment for their sins?

Verses 12-17: **Then came the word of the Lord unto Jeremiah,
saying, [13]Thus saith the Lord of hosts, the God of Israel; Go and tell
the men of Judah and the inhabitants of Jerusalem, Will ye not
receive instruction to hearken to my words? saith the Lord.
[14]The words of Jonadab the son of Rechab, that he commanded his
sons not to drink wine, are performed; for unto this day they drink
none, but obey their father's commandment: notwithstanding I have
spoken unto you, rising early and speaking; but ye hearkened not
unto me. [15]I have sent also unto you all my servants the prophets,
rising up early and sending them, saying, Return ye now every man
from his evil way, and amend your doings, and go not after other
gods to serve them, and ye shall dwell in the land which I have given
to you and to your fathers: but ye have not inclined your ear, nor
hearkened unto me. [16]Because the sons of Jonadab the son of
Rechab have performed the commandment of their father, which he
commanded them; but this people hath not hearkened unto me:
[17]Therefore thus saith the Lord God of hosts, the God of Israel;
Behold, I will bring upon Judah and upon all the inhabitants of
Jerusalem all the evil that I have pronounced against them: because
I have spoken unto them, but they have not heard; and I have called
unto them, but they have not answered.**

At the time, God did not explain to Jeremiah why the prophet was asked to offer wine to the Rechabites. Jeremiah may have wondered. The reason became clear when **the word of the Lord** came a second time **unto Jeremiah.** Using His full title, **the Lord of hosts, the God of Israel,** He gave Jeremiah the message he was to deliver to **the men of Judah and the inhabitants of Jerusalem.** The first part of the message was a question, **Will ye not receive instruction to hearken to my words?** "Will you not learn a lesson and obey my words?" (NIV). In Hebrew thought and language, to hear God was to obey God. Those who do not obey have not really heard. They heard the words and probably understood them, but they had not heeded the words.

Part of God's message to the people of Judah was to report on the continuing obedience of the Rechabites to the commands of Jonadab. We don't know how familiar the common people were with the Rechabites. Very likely, many people were aware of this nomadic group who lived in the land. They may have known of their strange ways and perhaps knew the history of the group. Perhaps the people were familiar with the Rechabites because they had come into Jerusalem seeking protection because of the dangerous political events that were happening. At any rate, Jeremiah told the people of Jerusalem of what Jonadab had taught and how the Rechabites had passed the test of integrity by refusing the wine that the prophet offered to them. Jeremiah used their obedience to their long-deceased forefather to contrast the disobedience of Judah to their God.

God listed the many and persistent ways He had tried to call His people to repentance and obedience. The Rechabites obeyed the teachings of a distant human ancestor. The people of Judah had turned a deaf ear to the pleas of their God. God's persistence is seen in the words **I have spoken unto you, rising early and speaking.** In spite of this loving persistence, the people **hearkened not unto** Him.

Verse 15 is one of those Bible verses that reveal the broken heart of a loving Father for His wayward children. The Lord sent His **servants the prophets** with this message and invitation: **Return ye now every man from his evil way, and amend your doings.** As far as God was concerned, He was eager to welcome those who turned from their sins to love and serve the Lord. Some people think of sin as a brave human struggle with an uncaring Deity, but it is actually a sin against a loving Father who yearns for the sinner's return. God, speaking through Ezekiel, gave this plaintive call: "Say to them, 'As surely as I live, declares the Sovereign LORD, I take no pleasure in the death of the wicked, but rather that they turn from their ways and live. Turn! Turn from your evil ways! Why will you die, O house of Israel?'" (Ezek. 33:11, NIV).

Jeremiah and Ezekiel were prophets during the final days of Judah, before the nation fell to the Babylonians. They preached repentance, but they lived to see their warnings of punishment come to pass. The people of Judah refused to repent and obey their God. This is the heart of human sin. "Obedience to the Lord's commands is not a problem unique to the Hebrews. From the beginning of history the human race has insisted on asserting its independence from God. It has not yet learned the lesson that declaring one's independence from God does not bring happiness or blessing that the tempter promises (see Gen. 3:5)."[2]

Verses 16-17 point to the tragic end of Judah because of disobedience and rejection of offers of God's love and forgiveness. Verse 16 again contrasted the obedience of the Rechabites to their ancestor Jonadab with the disobedience of Judah to God. Verse 17 spells out the warning that God will **bring upon Judah and upon all the inhabitants of Jerusalem all the evil that** He had **pronounced against them.** The judgment came in 587/586 B.C. when Nebuchadnezzar conquered Judah.

What are the lasting lessons of verses 12-17?

1. God uses godly families to be examples to others.
2. God pleads with sinners to repent and be saved.
3. God warns the disobedient of the dire consequences of their sins.
4. Too many people fail to hear and to heed God's Word.

Enjoy the Blessings of Obedience (Jer. 35:18-19)

What message did Jeremiah deliver to the Rechabites? How was this message good news for them?

Verses 18-19: **And Jeremiah said unto the house of the Rechabites, Thus saith the LORD of hosts, the God of Israel; Because ye have obeyed the commandment of Jonadab your father, and kept all his precepts, and done according unto all that he hath commanded you: 19therefore thus saith the LORD of hosts, the God of Israel; Jonadab the son of Rechab shall not want a man to stand before me forever.**

Verses 12-17 were directed to the people of Judah using the Rechabites as examples. Verses 18-19 close this incident with God's words of blessing to the Rechabites. If Jeremiah had been puzzled by God's command to offer wine to them, the Rechabites themselves must have been even more puzzled. Now they saw God's purpose. He did not want them to drink the wine and go against the heritage of their family. God wanted to use their loyalty as a message to Judah. Verses 18-19 leave no doubt about God's attitude toward them and their commitment not to drink wine.

The Lord commended them because they had **obeyed the commandment of Jonadab** their **father, and kept all his precepts, and done according unto all that he** had **commanded.** Then God promised them a blessing. This blessing is spelled out in the last part of verse 19: **Jonadab the son of Rechab shall not want a man to stand before me forever** ("will never fail to have a man to serve me," NIV). "The Hebrew says literally 'will not be cut off to stand before me all the days' (cf. a similar blessing on the descendants of David and the Levites, 33:17-18). 'Stand before me' is an expression that can mean *to stand before someone with an attitude of service.* It is found over one hundred times in the OT and is used of prophets (1 Kings 17:1), priests (Num. 16:9), and kings (1 Kings 10:8). . . . The blessing is a promise that they would not be destroyed as a family. Nehemiah 3:14 mentions a descendant of Rechab approximately 150 years later who was faithfully serving the Lord."[3]

A godly family experiences the blessings of God. These blessings are not arbitrarily given. They grow out of obedience to God. Such families know the assurance of God's love and presence. Although family members of each generation die, the family heritage continues. Blessed indeed are those born into a family with a heritage of faith and obedience. Blessed are the ones who pass this heritage on to their children and grandchildren.

What are the lasting lessons of verses 18-19?

1. God commends families who practice obedience to Him and respect and loyalty to a godly heritage.

2. God blesses such families.

❖ *Spiritual Transformations*

God told Jeremiah to offer wine to the Rechabites, a family whose ancestor Jonadab taught them not to drink wine, build houses, or plant vineyards. The Rechabites were obedient to their heritage and refused the wine. God told Jeremiah to use the Rechabites' obedience to their forefather's command as a contrast to the people of Judah, who disobeyed their God. The Lord promised the Rechabites that their family would continue to serve Him.

The impact of this lesson on your life can help you be a Jonadab in your family. Your family needs to be a family of faith and obedience. You can do your part to establish such a family. If you have been blessed with such a heritage, you can and need to pass it on to your children. In either case, you can help your family to be a good example to other people and families.

How do you evaluate the heritage you have received from your family? ____

If you need to establish a Christian home, what steps do you need to take? ____

If you have a godly heritage, how will you pass it on to others?

____

Prayer of Commitment: Lord, help me to do my part to make my home a Christian home. Amen.

[1]Chester Swor, *Very Truly Yours* [Nashville: Broadman Press, 1954], 46.

[2]F. B. Huey, Jr., "Jeremiah, Lamentations," in *The New American Commentary*, vol. 16 [Nashville: Broadman Press, 1993], 317.

[3]Huey, "Jeremiah, Lamentations," NAC, 317.

Week of May 11

MAKING PEACE IN MY FAMILY

Background Passage: Genesis 13:1-18
Focal Passage: Genesis 13:1-2,5-18
Key Verse: Genesis 13:8

❖ *Significance of the Lesson*

• The *Theme* of this lesson is that families who work together to have peace please God.

• The *Life Question* this lesson seeks to address is, How can I promote peace within my family?

• The *Biblical Truth* is that by relying on the Lord, family members can work together to settle conflicts peaceably.

• The *Life Impact* is to help you work for peace in your family.

Family Strife and Peace

In the secular worldview, self-fulfillment often takes precedence over the self-giving needed to have harmony in a family. Often conflicts over possessions are a key factor in strife within families. Strife is common in families, often with disastrous consequences. Among these are divorce, alienation, and abuse.

In the biblical worldview, family members seek to live at peace with one another. When potential strife arises, they seek to defuse it. When strife occurs, they seek reconciliation. Generosity and self-giving are keys to family peace. Reliance on God is essential.

Word Study: *strife*

The English word "strife" is found twice in Genesis 13:7-8 in the *King James Version* (and NASB), but each verse contains a different Hebrew word. The word in verse 7 is *rib*, a common word for "dispute," "argument," or "contention." The word in verse 8 is *m^{e}riba*, a less common word with similar meaning and the same root. *Rib* can refer to verbal strife (Ps. 31:20, "the strife of tongues") and it can refer to physical strife (Ps. 55:9, "violence and strife"). The *New*

International Version translates *rib* and *m^e^riba* as "quarreling." These translations assume that at this point in the problem the strife had not moved beyond verbal quarreling but that Abram feared it could escalate into physical violence.

❖ *Search the Scriptures*

When strife developed between the herdsmen of Abram and Lot, Abram proposed that they go to different areas in order to avoid further strife. He gave Lot the privilege of choosing which area he wanted. Lot decided on the rich Jordan Valley, which contained the wicked city of Sodom. God promised to give Abram the land and innumerable descendants.

The three points in the Focal Passage Outline are ways to achieve the Life Impact of helping you work for peace in your family.

Demonstrate Generosity (Gen. 13:1-2,5-9)

*What had happened to Abram in Egypt? Why was Lot traveling with him? Why was each man rich? What was a bad consequence of their wealth? What caused the **strife**? What commitment did Abram make to Lot? What plan did he offer? What basic principles for dealing with family strife do these verses illustrate?*

Verses 1-2: **And Abram went up out of Egypt, he, and his wife, and all that he had, and Lot with him, into the south. [2]And Abram was very rich in cattle, in silver, and in gold.**

Abram came **up out of Egypt.** Genesis 12:10-20 tells why he went to Egypt and what he did there. He went because of famine in Canaan. His behavior there was a low point in his life. He lied to Pharaoh and involved his wife Sarai in the deception. He told the ruler that she was his sister, for he feared for his life if Pharaoh knew this woman was his wife. By thinking of his own safety, he put Sarai at risk when Pharaoh brought her to his harem. Only after God sent trouble on Pharaoh did Pharaoh confront Abram, who finally confessed the truth. This incident shows that Abram was not perfect. In spite of this, God continued to bless him.

Lot was with Abram when he came out of Egypt and journeyed **into the south.** This doesn't mean that they went south from Egypt, but that when they returned to Canaan they headed for the southern part of the land called "the Negev" (NIV). Lot was the son of Abram's brother Haran, who died in Ur before the family went to the city of Haran. The family also included Terah, who was the father of Haran, Abram, and Nahor. After Terah's death, Abram answered God's call and ended up in Canaan. Lot went with him. The Bible does not tell us to what degree, if any, Lot shared the vision and faith of his uncle at that time. We can hope that Lot went with his uncle because of faith of his own.

Both men were **rich** in livestock, and **Abram was very rich** also **in silver, and in gold.** This is the first Bible reference to anyone being **rich.** The Bible warns about the dangers in riches, but Abram is an example of a rich person who viewed his possessions as gifts and trusts from God. He avoided the sins of the rich. He did not gain his wealth in sinful ways. He did not idolize it. He was generous. He is the first example of tithing in the Bible (14:18-20).

After Abram returned to the land of Canaan, he went to Bethel and worshiped at an altar he had made earlier. There he renewed his faith by calling on the name of the Lord (13:3-4). Perhaps he asked forgiveness for what he had done in Egypt. No mention is made of Lot's worship, but Abram may have been praying for the entire family.

Verses 5-7: **And Lot also, which went with Abram, had flocks, and herds, and tents. [6]And the land was not able to bear them, that they might dwell together: for their substance was great, so that they could not dwell together. [7]And there was a strife between the herdmen of Abram's cattle and the herdmen of Lot's cattle: and the Canaanite and the Perizzite dwelled then in the land.**

Lot too **had flocks, and herds, and tents.** This wealth may have been his inheritance from his father or it may have come from his association with Abram. Possessions can be blessings, but they also can be the occasion for trouble. The livestock of the uncle and his nephew became so many that **the land was not able to bear** ("support," NIV) **them.** The result was **that they could not dwell together.** One evidence of this was the **strife** that erupted between **the herdmen** of the two men.

This reminds us that strife often threatens families. As far as we know, it had not yet infected the relation of Abram and Lot; however, strife among their workers was bound to strain their family ties. The causes of family strife are many and varied. Relations are fragile and under tensions of many kinds. Tensions always have the potential for strife and its dire consequences. Certain tensions are normal in the best of families. For example, some tension exists when children pass through adolescence to adult status. These tensions can lead to strife if all family members do not work together to make this transition as smooth as possible. Adjustments in marriage are necessary as the nature of the relationship passes through its many stages. Family members do not always agree; therefore, they need to have some guidelines for handling potential strife.

Tensions can develop into actual strife. These can infect all kinds of family relationships: between spouses, between parents and children, between siblings, and between members of the extended family. The strife is often verbal, but sometimes it becomes physical. The consequences include alienation, divorce, and abuse of all kinds. Strife in families is always serious and dangerous. It makes members of the family miserable. When it happens in a believing family, it is a bad example to nonbelievers. In Abram's and Lot's day, **the Canaanite and the Perizzite** [PEHR-ih-zight] would have seen any strife between them.

Verses 8-9: **And Abram said unto Lot, Let there be no strife, I pray thee, between me and thee, and between my herdmen and thy herdmen; for we be brethren. 9Is not the whole land before thee? separate thyself, I pray thee, from me: if thou wilt take the left hand, then I will go to the right; or if thou depart to the right hand, then I will go to the left.**

Abram pleaded with Lot. He said, **Let there be no strife, I pray thee, between me and thee.** He went on also to mention strife **between** their **herdmen.** The **herdmen** already were engaged in **strife,** but apparently it had not yet involved the uncle and his nephew. Abram asked Lot to join him in a commitment to end strife and avoid future strife, especially between the two of them. He gave as his reason that **we be brethren.** They were not literally brothers, but they were members of the same family ("close relatives," CEV).

Abram wanted to stop the problem from moving to the next level. Apparently the strife between herdsmen was still only verbal at this time. Abram wanted to stop it before it led to physical strife. (See "Word Study.")

Abram's commitment to avoid strife applies to every family member, no matter what the relationship. Such a commitment is essential in relationships between spouses, between parents and children, between siblings, and all the others. Every effort should be used to avoid strife and to seek reconciliation if strife occurs. Strife is not the same thing as disagreements, although disagreements can degenerate into angry arguments and these can lead to even worse strife. One of the essentials of a lasting and happy marriage is learning to deal with conflict of opinions before it becomes dissension and strife. Conflict resolution is a skill that must be learned and practiced. No relations are so crucial as family relationships, and none require more love, forgiveness, forbearance, and patience. Paul's words to the family of faith apply also to the biological family: "Let not the sun go down upon your wrath. . . . Be ye kind one to another, tenderhearted, forgiving one another, even as God for Christ's sake hath forgiven you" (Eph. 4:26,32).

Abram not only made a commitment to and a plea for avoiding strife, but he also acted to make this possible. Although, as the elder of the two, he had the right to the best land, Abram chose to give that right to his nephew. Even though God had promised Abram **the whole land,** Abram allowed Lot to live in whatever part he chose. If Lot chose to **take the left hand,** Abram would **go to the right.** If Lot chose to **depart to the right hand,** Abram would **go to the left.**

This offer shows the generosity, humility, and self-giving of Abram. Some of the land was more suited to graze livestock; therefore, the choice had economic consequences. Thus Abram was generous in allowing Lot to make the choice. Possessions often are key factors in family disputes (Luke 12:13-15). Abram was rich, but he made family peace more important than gaining more wealth. He would have agreed with Proverbs 15:16-17:

> Better a little with the fear of the Lord
> than great wealth with turmoil.
> Better a meal of vegetables where there is love
> than a fatted calf with hatred (NIV).

Abram also was humble in stepping aside and allowing another to go first. He showed a spirit of self-giving love for his nephew. Families in which self-fulfillment is the primary goal set themselves up for strife. Only those who give of themselves unselfishly can have a family where peace and love prevail.

Abram was a peacemaker. He took the initiative in seeking to end the strife. Often when strife occurs, both parties are hurt and angry. Each one waits for the other to reach out and seek reconciliation. Pride keeps many family disputes alive for years. Alienated family members sometimes refuse to speak to one another, or they never speak words of love and concern for the other person. One of the saddest tragedies is when someone dies before things are made right with family members. Love needs to be expressed now. Jesus said to take the initiative in disputes whether your brother has a complaint against you (Matt. 5:23-24) or you have a complaint against your brother (18:15-17).

What are the lasting lessons in verses 1-2,5-9?

1. Some tensions are normal in families, but tensions can lead to angry disputes.

2. Angry disputes can lead to alienation or abuse that goes beyond words.

3. Believers should commit themselves to avoiding strife and to nurturing peace.

4. Christian love calls for the believer to take the initiative in resolving alienating strife.

5. Avoiding or resolving strife calls for humility and self-giving love.

6. Unbelievers observe how Christian families deal with tensions and strife.

Reject Selfishness (Gen. 13:10-13)

What options did Lot have? Why are decisions so crucial? Why did Lot make the decision he did? How do you evaluate Lot's character?

Verses 10-13: **And Lot lifted up his eyes, and beheld all the plain of Jordan, that it was well watered everywhere, before the LORD destroyed Sodom and Gomorrah, even as the garden of the LORD, like the land of Egypt, as thou comest unto Zoar. 11Then Lot chose him all the plain of Jordan; and Lot journeyed east: and they separated themselves the one from the other. 12Abram dwelled in the land of Canaan, and Lot dwelled in the cities of the plain, and pitched his tent toward Sodom. 13But the men of Sodom were wicked and sinners before the LORD exceedingly.**

Lot had a decision to make. He could settle in any part of the land. Life is filled with decisions, and many of them are crucial. You are who you are to a great extent because of decisions you made in the past. Decisions you make now will determine who you will be in the future. Choices become habits. Habits become character. Character becomes destiny.

Lot looked toward **the plain of Jordan.** He saw that **it was well watered everywhere.** This of course was **before the LORD destroyed Sodom and Gomorrah.** That terrible judgment changed the geography of the area. When Lot viewed it, the area was like **the garden of the LORD** and like the most fertile areas of **Egypt.** In other words, it was well suited for grazing livestock. Since this was the source of Lot's wealth, the area seemed ideal. Thus Lot **chose . . . all the plain of Jordan. Lot journeyed east** from the hill country of Canaan. Abram stayed in the hill country of Canaan, but Lot **pitched his tent toward Sodom** ("put up his tents not far from Sodom," CEV).

What kind of man was Lot? Most Bible students interpret these verses as evidence that he was selfish, greedy, and ungrateful. He agreed with Abram that they should avoid strife by separating. He quickly chose for himself what appeared to be the better part of the land. An unselfish person would have recognized the self-giving of his uncle. At the very least, he could have thanked his uncle for giving him first choice. He might even have refused to make the decision and given it to Abram. However, even if he had, Abram might have chosen the hill country of Canaan. He and Lot didn't have the same values. Abram defined the better part of the land as something other than its potential for greater wealth. But Lot was defining the better choice in materialistic terms. He felt that he could get richer faster in that area.

Sodom is mentioned three times in verses 10-13, and each reference has a sense of coming doom. Its future destruction is mentioned in verse 10. Lot's moving toward Sodom, in which he soon dwelt (14:12), is mentioned in verse 12. He continued to stay there until the city was destroyed (chap. 19). Verse 13 states clearly the evil for which it was known: **The men of Sodom were wicked and sinners before the LORD exceedingly.** Sodom's reputation was well known throughout the land. Even if Lot did not know its wickedness when he made his choice, he soon would have discovered it. Yet he moved to Sodom knowing full well what it was like.

Actually, Lot's character is an enigma. Although chapter 19 is not in the Focal Passage, this is an important source for evaluating Lot. When the angels visited Sodom, Lot welcomed them. When the Sodomites came to his house and demanded that the two guests be given to them for sexual abuse, Lot refused and rebuked the mob at his door. This scene in Genesis 19:1-7 probably is the basis for the most positive thing the Bible says about Lot (in spite of his statement in v. 8). Second Peter 2:7 describes how God delivered Lot from Sodom's destruction: "He rescued Lot, a righteous man, who was distressed by the filthy lives of lawless men (for that righteous man, living among them day after day, was tormented in his righteous soul by the lawless deeds he saw and heard)" (NIV).

Although Lot was disturbed by the immorality of Sodom, he moved there and stayed there. When the angels told him to take his family and flee, they had to force him to leave Sodom behind (Gen. 19:16). W. H. Griffith Thomas wrote this analysis of Lot's character: "What a contrast between Lot and Abraham! Except for 2 Peter ii 7,8, we should have hardly credited Lot with any vital religion. Although 'righteous,' he is yet living by sight, seeking only his own advantages and pleasure; worldliness is his dominant characteristic, his one thought is the well-watered plains. He is a type and illustration of the Christian who is not fully consecrated—one who is trying to make the best of both worlds, endeavoring to stand well with God, while pushing to the full his own earthly interests."[1]

What lasting lessons are in verses 10-13?

1. Decisions at crucial times in life determine what kind of person each of us becomes.
2. Economic considerations should not be the dominant factors in decisions.
3. People of faith should avoid situations where evil is in control.

Rely on the Lord (Gen. 13:14-18)

How did Abram react to Lot's choice? Why are faith and obedience essential to claim God's best promises? Why did Abram and Lot see different things when they lifted up their eyes? What is the significance of Abram building an altar?

Verses 14-18: **And the Lord said unto Abram, after that Lot was separated from him, Lift up now thine eyes, and look from the place where thou art northward, and southward, and eastward, and westward: 15 for all the land which thou seest, to thee will I give it, and to thy seed forever. 16 And I will make thy seed as the dust of the earth: so that if a man can number the dust of the earth, then shall thy seed also be numbered. 17 Arise, walk through the land in the length of it and in the breadth of it; for I will give it unto thee.**

18Then Abram removed his tent, and came and dwelt in the plain of Mamre, which is in Hebron, and built there an altar unto the LORD.

And the LORD said unto Abram shows that the Lord spoke to Abram. The words here are the first recorded words of the Lord to Abram since Genesis 12:7, when Abram first arrived in Canaan. God may have chosen this time to speak to Abram because Abram needed the encouragement only God could give him.

Thus it was **that Lot was separated from him.** True to his word, Abram allowed Lot to choose the part of the land he wanted. He and Lot had been together for a long time, so he must have missed his nephew. Although they were separated, Abram continued to keep up with Lot. When Lot was taken captive, his uncle rescued him (14:1-16). When the Lord told Abraham of the coming ruin of Sodom, Abraham interceded for the city (18:16-33). After the Lord delivered Lot from Sodom's destruction, the Bible says it was because of Abraham (19:29).

When God told Abram, **Lift up now thine eyes,** He used the same expression as is used of Lot's action in verse 10. But when Lot **lifted up his eyes,** he saw things very differently than Abram did. Lot looked with covetous eyes on the fertile valley and saw a vision of greater wealth for himself. Abram lifted up his eyes and saw the vision of what God promised to him. Lot viewed life from a worldly perspective. Abram viewed life through the eyes of faith.

God enlarged upon the promise of Genesis 12:7. God asked Abram to look to the north, south, east, and west. The Lord promised to give all the land Abram could see to him and to his **seed** ("offspring," NIV) **forever.** God promised that Abram's offspring would be as numerous **as the dust of the earth.** Lot had laid claim to one area, which soon was devastated. Abram was to receive the whole land. In order to lay claim to this promise, God told Abram to **walk through the land in the length of it and in the breadth of it.** God's best blessings must be appropriated by faith and obedience. God's promise to Abram was sealed by Abram's obedience in walking throughout the land.

Lot had **pitched his tent toward Sodom.** His uncle **removed his tent, and came and dwelt in the plain of Mamre, which is in Hebron, and built there an altar unto the LORD.** This is the third time it is recorded that Abram worshiped at **an altar unto the LORD.** When he arrived in Canaan, he built an altar and called on the name of the Lord (12:8). When he came back from Egypt, he went back to that altar and called on the name of the Lord (13:3-4). Now after Lot had left, he **built . . . an altar unto the Lord.** Abram was a person of genuine faith. Such people always maintain a vital relation to the Lord through worship and prayer.

Abram trusted in the Lord to keep His promises. He did not rely on his wealth or on his ability, but he relied on the Lord. Families must learn to rely on the Lord. A young couple was talking about marriage. Someone asked them what visible means of support they had. A better question might be to inquire what invisible means of support they have in terms of their faith in God.

What are the lasting lessons of verses 14-18?

1. God speaks to us if we are listening.
2. Believers view life through eyes of faith.
3. God's best promises are appropriated by faith and obedience.
4. We can rely on God's promises.
5. We must maintain a vital relation to God.

❖ *Spiritual Transformations*

When Abram heard of quarreling between his herdsman and Lot's herdsmen, he proposed that he and Lot act to avoid strife between the two of them. He gave Lot the choice of the area where he would live. Lot chose the rich plain of the Jordan Valley and moved his tent near Sodom. God promised Abram to give to him and his offspring the land. Abram built an altar and worshiped the Lord.

One of the goals of families is peace. The biblical view of peace is more than the absence of strife. The biblical understanding of peace also involves each person having peace with God, with one another, and within themselves. A family, therefore, should provide a place where each person can become what God wants the person to be.

*What strife or potential strife in your family do you need to deal with?*____

*What can you do to promote peace in your family?*________________

____

Prayer of Commitment: Lord, help me do my part to avoid strife and to have peace in my family. Amen.

[1]W. H. Griffith Thomas, *Genesis: A Devotional Commentary* [Grand Rapids: William B. Eerdmans Publishing Company, 1946], 125.

Week of May 18

GIVING UNSELFISHLY TO GOD'S WORK

Bible Passage: Acts 4:32–5:11
Key Verse: Acts 4:32

❖ *Significance of the Lesson*

• The *Theme* of this lesson is that families with a right attitude toward giving honor God.

• The *Life Question* this lesson seeks to address is, With what attitudes should I and my family give to God's work?

• The *Biblical Truth* is that Christian families should give to God's work voluntarily, without duplicity, and out of reverence for God.

• The *Life Impact* is to help you develop a lifestyle of giving unselfishly to God's work.

Giving or Keeping?

In a secular worldview, a common attitude is to hoard or to spend rather than to give. Some who do give may do so to call attention to themselves.

In a biblical worldview, however, believers give unselfishly to God's work to honor Him and to meet the needs of others.

Word Study: *grace*

The word **grace** in Acts 4:33 translates *charis,* meaning "favor," "blessing," or "grace." This word was often used in greeting. Many New Testament letters begin with the twofold greeting of "grace" and "peace" (the latter being the usual Jewish greeting). The word **grace** is used for the unmerited love of God in saving sinners (Eph. 2:8-9). It is also used to indicate the favor of God on a person or group.

❖ *Search the Scriptures*

The Jerusalem church gave generously and voluntarily to meet the needs of those in the congregation. Barnabas is a positive example.

Ananias and Sapphira are negative examples. They lied to the Holy Spirit and fell dead when confronted with their sin. The result was a sense of holy fear among those who learned of this event.

The three Focal Passage Outline points answer the Life Question, With what attitudes should I and my family give to God's work?

Give Voluntarily (Acts 4:32-37)

What characteristics of the Jerusalem church are found in these verses? What was distinctive about their giving? How do we know that this was voluntary giving? What kind of person was Joseph? What are the lasting principles from the sharing that occurred in this church?

Acts 4:32-35: **And the multitude of them that believed were of
one heart and of one soul: neither said any of them that ought of
the things which he possessed was his own; but they had all things
common. 33And with great power gave the apostles witness of the
resurrection of the Lord Jesus: and great grace was upon them all.
34Neither was there any among them that lacked: for as many as
were possessors of lands or houses sold them, and brought the
prices of the things that were sold, 35and laid them down at the
apostles' feet: and distribution was made unto every man according
as he had need.**

Some of the verses in Acts 4:32-35 sound as if the Jerusalem church in the early years practiced a kind of community of possessions. A close study of these verses shows this is not an accurate understanding.

Enemies were persecuting the Jerusalem church. The believers had just passed through one of these threats (vv. 13-31). Part of their strength came from the strong fellowship in the church. They **were of one heart and of one soul.** The last part of verse 32 lists an important expression of this oneness—their sharing of possessions. Verse 32b says, "No one claimed that any of his possessions was his own" (NIV). This does not mean that no one continued to have anything of **his own.** It means that they did not show the kind of selfish spirit that some people use when they speak of their possessions.

When the world uses the word *mine,* they use it like a child does when he grabs a favorite toy, clutches it tightly, and says, "This is mine, not yours." Christian love demands that believers give of themselves and their possessions for the needs of others—"What's mine is yours." Those who have oneness of Spirit in the Lord have a sense of belonging to the Lord and to one another. One expression of this oneness is giving to meet the needs of others.

Common translates *koinos,* a word that is kin to *koinonia,* which describes the oneness of the church in Christ. Believers have in common their relationship to the same Lord. Because of having Christ in common, those in the Jerusalem church considered all they possessed to be in common. They may have had a common fund into which voluntary gifts were put and from which distributions were made, but the common fund did not contain all the possessions of all the members.

Verse 33 deals with the outreach of the church. **The apostles** continued to proclaim **the resurrection of the Lord Jesus** and they did so **with great power.** The **power,** of course, was that of the Spirit of God. Including verse 33a in the midst of a description of the giving of the early church shows that oneness of spirit is not inconsistent with an evangelistic spirit. In fact, in the New Testament, evangelism and fellowship are inseparable. A church should be a warm fellowship, but it must not become a closed society that is content with itself. The warmer the family spirit, the warmer should be the outreach for others. A Sunday School class ought to be a support group, but it must not become exclusive instead of inclusive.

The words **great grace was upon them all** reinforce that the sharing of goods and proclaiming Christ were acts made possible by the grace of God. They had been saved by God's grace, and His favor rested on them and inspired them as they lived for Him and served Him. These words show that God's favor rested on them. He was pleased with what they were doing.

The background to verse 34a is Deuteronomy 15:1-11. **Neither was there any among them that lacked** sounds like the ideal situation described in Deuteronomy 15:4: "There shall be no poor among you."

The last part of verse 34 and the first part of verse 35 sound as if every church member gave everything to the common fund: **As many as were possessors of lands or houses sold them, and brought the prices of the things that were sold, and laid them down at the apostles' feet.** But the tense of the verbs describe continuous actions. The *New International Version*'s "from time to time" is an attempt to indicate this. Charles R. Erdman wrote of the giving in the Jerusalem church: "The 'community of goods' here described was purely local, temporary, occasional, and voluntary. It was practiced only in Jerusalem, not in other cities of the empire, and there only for a time.

It was not observed by all Christians even in Jerusalem, in the sense that all their possessions were sold and placed in a common fund. . . . The facts seem to be that many Christians did contribute to the treasury of the Church all they had, others sold their possessions from time to time as special demands for relief arose, still others retained the ownership of their property regarding it as a sacred trust."[1]

In the words **distribution was made unto every man according as he had need,** the word **need** is important. The Greek word is *chreia.* This word can refer to needs in general, but it usually refers to someone who was poor enough to be dependent on others. This is the word used in 1 John 3:17, where we read, "If anyone has material possessions and sees his brother in need but has no pity on him, how can the love of God be in him?" (NIV). The church was as careful as possible in determining who had real economic needs. Therefore, the Jerusalem church did not use its common fund to provide for the economic needs of all the members (as they would have if everyone had put everything in the common pool). They used it to help the truly needy.

No other New Testament church had a program exactly like the one in Jerusalem; however, the basic principles apply to all churches. Therefore, we need to distinguish what was unique to Jerusalem from principles that all of us should practice. The unique thing was the total commitment to meet the needs of poor church members by other members selling some possession and using the money to help the needy.

Acts 4:36-37: **And Joses, who by the apostles was surnamed Barnabas, (which is, being interpreted, The son of consolation,) a Levite, and of the country of Cyprus, [37]having land, sold it, and brought the money, and laid it at the apostles' feet.**

Joses is the Greek form of the name "Joseph" (NIV, HCSB). Joseph was a famous name in the Bible, but this man was known more by his nickname. **The apostles** called him **Barnabas.** This name means **son of consolation. Consolation** translates *paraklesis,* which means "encouragement" (NIV, HCSB). In most of the biblical stories about Barnabas, he was encouraging others. He encouraged Saul of Tarsus when he stood up for the former persecutor before the leaders of the Jerusalem church (9:26-27). He encouraged the new approaches of the church at Antioch (11:22-26). He encouraged John Mark by giving him a second chance (15:36-41). Here in Acts 4:36-39 he encouraged the poor in Jerusalem by his generous gift. He is cited as a good example of how one person practiced verses 32-35. Barnabas owned some **land,** which he **sold.** Then he **brought the money, and laid it at the apostles' feet.**

This was a voluntary and generous gift. It shows that Barnabas owned something that he chose to sell and to give the money to the apostles. We are not told whether he owned other land, but he gave something that he could have kept for future security or profit. Many people think they never get enough for themselves. One secret of generous giving is contentment with less than others think is necessary for the good life and for security.

In laying the proceeds **at the apostles' feet,** Barnabas was giving it to God for use in helping the needy. The apostles, in receiving his gift, were accountable for distributing it in the way Barnabas intended.

Barnabas is mentioned as a good example to others of generous giving. In a family, parents set an example for their children by how they deal with possessions. Some set a bad example. Others teach generosity by how they give.

What are the lasting lessons in Acts 4:32-37?

1. Bold witnessing and warm fellowship are inseparable.
2. Christian giving is an expression of oneness in Christ.
3. Christian giving is voluntary.
4. Christian giving is generous.
5. Generous giving pleases God.
6. Generous giving sets a good example.
7. Christian giving meets the needs of others.

Give Without Duplicity (Acts 5:1-4)

Why did Ananias sell the field? Why did he hold back some of the selling price? How involved was Sapphira in this decision? What was Ananias's sin? What part did Satan play?

Acts 5:1-4: **But a certain man named Ananias, with Sapphira his
wife, sold a possession, 2and kept back part of the price, his wife also
being privy to it, and brought a certain part, and laid it at the apostles' feet. 3But Peter said, Ananias, why hath Satan filled thine heart
to lie to the Holy Ghost** [Spirit], **and to keep back part of the price of
the land? 4Whiles it remained, was it not thine own? and after it was
sold, was it not in thine own power? why hast thou conceived this
thing in thine heart? thou hast not lied unto men, but unto God.**

The account of **Ananias** and **Sapphira** begins, as did the account of Barnabas, by stating that they **sold a possession.** However, they were the opposite kind of people from Barnabas. Barnabas acted for the glory of God and to meet the needs of others. Although the text does not spell out their motives, the context implies that Ananias and Sapphira acted in order to be praised for their generosity.

Both husband and **wife** conspired together in what they did: "With his wife's full knowledge he kept back part of the money for himself" (NIV). Ananias and Sapphira were motivated by selfishness and covetousness. We aren't told whether keeping back part of the proceeds was their plan from the beginning or whether they decided to do this after they had the money from the sale. In either case, they kept part for themselves. Then Ananias **brought a certain part, and laid it at the apostles' feet.** This action, on the surface, appeared to mimic what Barnabas had done. In other words, what he brought was supposed to be the total selling price. Later, when Sapphira came, Peter asked her if they had brought all the money from the sale.

When Ananias came, Peter knew that he had not brought it all. **Peter** asked Ananias why he had kept **back part of the price of the land.** Verse 4 again shows that the Jerusalem believers' giving was voluntary giving of their private property. The possession was theirs to sell or to keep. Further, they were free to give whatever part they chose to give. But Ananias was claiming before the church to be giving the entire selling price. To do this was **to lie to the Holy Ghost** ("Spirit," NIV, HCSB). There was no sin in selling the field or even in keeping part of it, but they sinned by claiming to offer all to the Lord, when they brought only part. **Lie** translates *pseudomai.* John B. Polhill noted that it might also be translated "belie" or "falsify." "Peter accused Ananias of lying to the Spirit. The Greek expression is even stronger than that—he 'belied,' he 'falsified' the Spirit. His action was in effect a denial, a falsification of the Spirit's presence in the community."[2] Ananias certainly lied. He claimed to be led by the Spirit, but Satan actually led him. Peter asked Ananias why he had let **Satan** fill his **heart.**

This was a serious sin against God. Lying to God is both foolish and sinful. Claiming to be led by the Spirit when actually led by the devil is even worse.

What are the lasting lessons of Acts 5:1-4?

1. Don't give to God in order to be praised by other people.
2. Don't act out of covetousness.
3. Don't lie to or falsify the Holy Spirit.

Give Out of Reverence for God (Acts 5:5-11)

Why did Ananias die? Why was he buried so soon? How did Peter give Sapphira an opportunity to confess? What was her sin? Were Ananias and Sapphira true believers? What effect did the news of these deaths have on others?

Acts 5:5-11: **And Ananias hearing these words fell down, and gave up the ghost: and great fear came on all them that heard these**
things. 6And the young men arose, wound him up, and carried him
out, and buried him. 7And it was about the space of three hours
after, when his wife, not knowing what was done, came in. 8And
Peter answered unto her, Tell me whether ye sold the land for so
much? And she said, Yea, for so much. 9Then Peter said unto her,
How is it that ye have agreed together to tempt the Spirit of the Lord? behold, the feet of them which have buried thy husband are
at the door, and shall carry thee out. 10Then fell she down straightway at his feet, and yielded up the ghost: and the young men came in, and found her dead, and, carrying her forth, buried her by her
husband. 11And great fear came upon all the church, and upon as many as heard these things.

When **Ananias** heard Peter speak **these words** of verses 3-4, he **fell down, and gave up the ghost.** The Greek behind **gave up the ghost** actually is only one word: "he died" *(exepsuxen).* What caused Ananias's death? Some feel he died of shock with a heart attack. Whatever the autopsy report would have said, his death was a judgment from God. The same Greek word for death is used in 12:23 for the evil Herod Agrippa, but there it is explicitly said, "the angel of the Lord smote him." In that land and time, people were usually buried on the day of their death. Thus "the young men came forward, wrapped up his body, and carried him out and buried him" (NIV).

For some reason that we are not told, **his wife** came in about **three hours** later. Peter asked her if they had sold the field for the amount of money they had brought. Peter seems to have been giving her an opportunity to tell the truth. Instead of confessing their sin, she told a bold-faced lie. She apparently had not heard of her husband's death. Peter shocked her by asking, **How is it that ye have agreed together to tempt** ("test," NIV, HCSB) **the Spirit of the Lord?** Peter knew that the couple had conspired together. Peter pronounced her judgment when he told her, "The feet of the men who buried your husband are at the door, and they will carry you out also" (NIV). She fell dead on the spot, and the young men took her body out and buried it.

When Ananias died in the way he did, **great fear came on all them that heard these things** (v. 5). When the same thing happened to his wife, **great fear came upon all the church, and upon as many as heard these things** (v. 11). The Bible, especially the Old Testament, calls on people to fear the Lord. Although love dominates in the New Testament, the New Testament also warns of the deadliness of sin and calls sinners to fear the Lord. The author of Hebrews 10:31 wrote, "It is a fearful thing to fall into the hands of the living God." For people of faith and obedience, being in God's hands is a reassuring experience; however, for those who disobey, it is a fearful thing. Biblical fear includes awe and reverence, but it also includes fear of punishment for sin.

Were Ananias and Sapphira true believers? They may have been believers who were guilty of serious sins. If so, they were saved but as through fire (1 Cor. 3:15). God sometimes punishes sins of believers with illness and even with death (11:30). Or they may have been church members but not true believers. Either way, they committed serious sins and were punished quickly. What would happen today if God were to smite with death all church members who committed the sins Ananias and Sapphira committed?

What are the lasting lessons of Acts 5:5-11?

1. Sin is serious because it is against God.
2. God sometimes quickly punishes people for their sins.
3. Fear of the Lord is a healthy response to His judgments.

❖ *Spiritual Transformations*

The Jerusalem church expressed its oneness in Christ by sharing their possessions with the poor. Barnabas is a good example of someone who did this. Ananias and Sapphira are negative examples. They sinned by lying to the Holy Spirit. When they fell dead, fear came on the church and on all who heard of it.

The lessons in this Study Theme focus on the family. The principles of giving in this lesson apply to individuals and to families. Parents should set good examples for their children by being generous and faithful stewards of their possessions. Their gifts to God should be given voluntarily, without duplicity, and out of reverence for God—and they should teach their children to do likewise.

What kind of example of Christian giving are you? ______________

____

In what ways do you need to improve? ______________

____

Prayer of Commitment: Lord, help me to be a generous giver and to set a good example for my family. Amen.

[1]Charles R. Erdman, *The Acts* [Philadelphia: The Westminster Press, 1936], 47-48.

[2]John B. Polhill, "Acts," in *The New American Commentary*, vol. 26 [Nashville: Broadman Press, 1992], 157.

Week of May 25

SERVING GOD TOGETHER AS A FAMILY

Background Passage: Acts 18:1-28; Romans 16:3-5;
1 Corinthians 16:19

**Focal Passage: Acts 18:1-4,24-28; Romans 16:3-5a;
1 Corinthians 16:19**

Key Verse: Acts 18:26

❖ *Significance of the Lesson*

• The *Theme* of the lesson is that families can work together to serve God.

• The *Life Question* this lesson seeks to address is, How can my family serve God together?

• The *Biblical Truth* is that believers can serve God together as a family.

• The *Life Impact* is to help you regularly serve God with family members.

Families and Service to God

In the secular world, many families are fragmented. Even family members living in the same household often are at odds with one another. Secular families give no thought to serving God.

In the biblical worldview, families recognize their need to know and serve God. They experience unity and fulfillment as they serve God together.

Word Study: *helpers*

The word translated **helpers** in Romans 16:3 is *synergous.* This combines the prefix *syn,* which means "together with," and *ergon,* which means "work." The word can be translated "fellow workers" or "coworkers." Paul often used the word to describe various ones of his fellow workers. He used it in Romans 16:3 to describe Aquila and Priscilla. He used the same word for Timothy (v. 21), Epaphroditus [ih-paf-roh-DIGH-tuhs] (Phil. 2:25), and others.

❖ *Search the Scriptures*

Paul stayed with Aquila and Priscilla and worked as a tentmaker as he also preached the good news in Corinth. This same couple were mentors to Apollos when he lacked full understanding of the gospel. Aquila and Priscilla risked their lives for Paul. They opened their house as a meeting place for the church in a couple of cities where they lived.

The four Focal Passage Outline points answer the Life Question, How can my family serve God together?

Labor with God's People (Acts 18:1-4)

What was Paul's situation when he went to Corinth? What do we know about Aquila and Priscilla? When did they become Christians? What was their relationship to Paul? How did Paul begin his work in Corinth?

Acts 18:1-4: **After these things Paul departed from Athens, and came to Corinth; [2]and found a certain Jew named Aquila, born in Pontus, lately come from Italy, with his wife Priscilla; (because that Claudius had commanded all Jews to depart from Rome:) and came unto them. [3]And because he was of the same craft, he abode with them, and wrought: for by their occupation they were tentmakers. [4]And he reasoned in the synagogue every sabbath, and persuaded the Jews and the Greeks.**

Paul was on his second missionary journey. He came from **Athens** to **Corinth.** His work in Athens had been difficult. He witnessed to the Greek philosophers with few positive results (17:16-34). He went to Corinth, which had challenges of its own. It was a seaport city and was notorious for the immoral lifestyle of its people. Paul seems to have arrived in Corinth alone. Silas and Timothy joined him only later. The fact that Paul worked in something other than preaching and teaching shows that he may have been short of funds at the time. So he faced the daunting mission to this wicked city alone and possibly while he was low on funds. He needed work, a place to stay, and some entree to the synagogue.

The word **found** implies that Paul was looking for work and lodging. He found both in the house of **Aquila** and **Priscilla.** We know from several of Paul's writings that he supported himself at times with his own work, but only here do we learn what his work was. He and Aquila had

the same craft. Their **occupation** is specified—**they were tentmakers.** The tents may have been of cloth or of leather. Although Paul had a formal education to be a teacher or rabbi, in those days a rabbi was expected also to have another way of making a living. Paul had learned how to make tents. This is probably how he and Aquila came together.

Aquila was **a certain Jew.** He had a Latin name. He was **born in Pontus,** an area in northern Asia Minor. At some point he moved to **Rome. Priscilla** was **his wife.** Her background is not given. She probably was also a Jew. The basis for this is the fact that they went to a synagogue (v. 26). They had moved to Corinth from Rome when **Claudius** expelled the Jews from that city. Claudius was emperor in A.D. 41-54. The Roman historian Suetonius wrote in his *Life of Claudius* that the reason for this action was a tumult over someone called "Chrestus" (a common misspelling for "Christ"). We do not know if Aquila and Priscilla became Christians before or after they met Paul.

Paul launched his missionary work in Corinth in his usual way: **He reasoned in the synagogue every sabbath, and persuaded the Jews and the Greeks.** As often happened, the majority of the synagogue opposed Paul, and he was forced to move elsewhere and to focus on the Gentiles. In Corinth, Paul moved next door from the synagogue to the house of a man named Justus. Crispus the ruler of the synagogue was converted and many of the Corinthians believed (see vv. 5-8). The Lord encouraged Paul in a vision, and he stayed in Corinth for 18 months (vv. 9-11). Leading Jews brought Paul to court, but Gallio the Roman deputy for Achaia, scorned them and their charges against Paul (vv. 12-14).

We are not told what part Aquila and Priscilla played in the actions of verses 4-14. Paul may or may not have spent 18 months in their house, but they were close enough to Paul that they went with him when he left Corinth (v. 18). This and other references to Aquila and Priscilla in Paul's letters show that they continued to work together with Paul and other believers.

Paul's friendship with Aquila and Priscilla show that he recognized the unique opportunities of a married couple in serving the Lord. Aquila and Priscilla were a family. We never read of any children, but in each reference to them both are mentioned. They lived and served together, and they served together with other believers. Thus they represent the basic principle of families working together with God's people.

What are the lasting lessons of Acts 18:1-4?

1. Members of a family should all be committed to Jesus Christ.
2. A Christian family practices hospitality.
3. A Christian family can help those called as missionaries and preachers.
4. A Christian husband and wife have many opportunities to serve the Lord together and to labor together with God's people.

Mentor Other Believers (Acts 18:24-28)

Why did Aquila and Priscilla go to Ephesus? Who was Apollos? What positive qualities did Apollos have? What was Apollos lacking? What did Aquila and Priscilla do to help Apollos? What does this reveal about them? What did the response of Apollos reveal about him?

Acts 18:24-28: **And a certain Jew named Apollos, born at Alexandria, an eloquent man, and mighty in the scriptures, came to Ephesus. 25This man was instructed in the way of the Lord; and being fervent in the spirit, he spake and taught diligently the things of the Lord, knowing only the baptism of John. 26And he began to speak boldly in the synagogue: whom when Aquila and Priscilla had heard, they took him unto them, and expounded unto him the way of God more perfectly. 27And when he was disposed to pass into Achaia, the brethren wrote, exhorting the disciples to receive him: who, when he was come, helped them much which had believed through grace: 28for he mightily convinced the Jews, and that publicly, showing by the scriptures that Jesus was Christ.**

The Book of Acts does not tell us why Aquila and Priscilla made the journey to **Ephesus** with Paul. They may have moved for business reasons, or they may have moved to provide a nucleus for a church in Ephesus. Paul was on his way to Antioch to report on his missionary work, but he stopped briefly in Ephesus. He preached in the synagogue, and they asked him to stay. He said that he could not stay, but he promised to return. Although Paul did not stay, his two fellow workers did stay (vv. 18-23). Later, Paul returned for one of his longest and most significant ministries. Meanwhile, Aquila and Priscilla carried on the witness in Ephesus until Paul returned.

Like Aquila, **Apollos** is introduced as **a certain Jew.** Apollos was **born at Alexandria.** He came to Ephesus as a preacher. Five positive qualities of his are mentioned. (1) He was **an eloquent man.** The Greek word rendered **eloquent** can mean "learned" (NIV). Apollos seems to have been both well educated and a good speaker. (2) He was **mighty in the scriptures. The scriptures** were the books of the Old Testament. One of his strengths was his "thorough knowledge of the Scriptures" (NIV). (3) Apollos was **fervent in the spirit.** This may refer to the Spirit of God or to his own spirit (as KJV). (4) He had been **instructed in the way of the Lord.** (5) He **taught diligently the things of the Lord. Diligently** translates the word *akribos,* which can mean either "accurately" or "carefully."

Yet as Aquila and Priscilla listened to this eloquent young man preach with zeal, they sensed that he lacked something. Luke stated that Apollos knew **only the baptism of John.** Bible students have various theories about what this meant in the life of Apollos. Some Bible students feel that Apollos knew nothing of the cross and resurrection or of Pentecost. Others think he only lacked a full understanding of Christian baptism. Still others think the Apollos knew nothing of the coming of the Spirit at Pentecost. John had said that he baptized with water but that the Messiah would baptize with the Holy Spirit.

Whatever it was that he lacked, Aquila and Priscilla had to decide what to do about it. They had three options. (1) They could ignore it. (2) They could criticize the young preacher. (3) They could try to help him. They chose to seek to help him—**they took him unto them** ("They invited him to their home," NIV). While he was there, they **expounded unto him the way of God more perfectly. More perfectly** translates *akribesteron,* the comparative form of *akribos.* Thus, although Apollos preached "the things about Jesus accurately," Aquila and Priscilla "explained the way of God to him more accurately" (HCSB).

What does this reveal about Aquila and Priscilla? They were mature in their own understanding and experience of the gospel. They had been with Paul long enough to learn what he believed and taught. They were committed to the Lord and to His work. They saw the potential in this gifted young man, and they wanted him to preach the full message. What Apollos said was accurate, but they were concerned about what he did not say. Therefore, for the sake of Apollos and those who heard him speak, they acted with courage and compassion by seeking to instruct the enthusiastic young preacher.

As in all their ventures, Aquila and Priscilla did this together. They were partners not only as husband and wife but also as fellow

Christians. Together they joined in seeking to instruct Apollos. And Apollos listened and learned from this couple, who probably lacked the educational credentials he had. Probably neither Aquila or Priscilla was an eloquent public speaker, yet Apollos recognized their sincerity and the truth of what they told him. He thus showed himself to be a humble person who was open to be taught.

After this meeting with Aquila and Priscilla, Apollos went on to be greatly used by the Lord. After serving in Ephesus, he wanted **to pass into Achaia.** The brothers in Ephesus **wrote** a letter commending him and **exhorting the disciples to receive him.**

Apollos went to Corinth (19:1). He **helped them much which had believed through grace.** In addition to this ministry to believers, **he mightily convinced** his fellow **Jews.** Later references to Apollos are found in Paul's letters. Some of the Corinthians sought to make Paul and Apollos into competitors for their allegiance, but Paul always spoke highly of Apollos (1 Cor. 1:12; 3:4-6; 4:6; 16:12; Titus 3:13).

In a very real sense, Aquila and Priscilla had a part in all that Apollos did. God used their help to equip Apollos for effective ministry.

Aquila and Priscilla were friends, helpers, teachers, and mentors. Apollos was blessed to have Aquila and Priscilla as his mentors. Who has been a mentor to you? Perhaps it was a pastor, a Sunday School teacher, or a Christian friend. I can think of several people who have been mentors to me. They went out of their way to help me learn and grow as a Christian.

Who is offering to be a mentor to you? None of us ever gets beyond needing the counsel of a friend. Are you following the example of Apollos in how you respond?

To whom are you acting as a mentor? What can you learn from the example of Aquila and Priscilla?

What are the lasting lessons in Acts 18:24-28?

1. Mature Christians can mentor others.
2. A couple can be partners in blessing and helping others.
3. A young, enthusiastic preacher can learn from dedicated lay people.
4. Being a mentor takes compassion, courage, and tact.
5. Learning from a mentor requires a humble and teachable attitude.
6. As believers, all of us at times need a mentor, and we need to be a mentor to others.

Demonstrate Self-Sacrifice (Rom. 16:3-4)

What shows Paul's continuing high regard for Aquila and Priscilla? What did it mean to be ***helpers in Christ Jesus****? When and how did Aquila and Priscilla risk their lives for Paul? How did Paul respond to their help? How well known was this couple?*

Romans 16:3-4: **Greet Priscilla and Aquila my helpers in Christ Jesus: [4]who have for my life laid down their own necks: unto whom not only I give thanks, but also all the churches of the Gentiles.**

When Paul wrote the Letter to the Romans, he had not been to Rome; however, he knew many of the members of the church. Romans 16 lists the names of members to whom Paul sent greetings. The first to be greeted were **Priscilla and Aquila.** This couple is mentioned six times in the New Testament—three times in Acts and three times in Paul's letters. They are always listed together. Here Priscilla's name is listed first. In the best Greek manuscripts of the New Testament, her name appears first in four of the six times they are mentioned. In Paul's letters, she is called by her formal name "Prisca." Priscilla, the diminutive form of Prisca, is used in the Book of Acts.

Paul called them his **helpers in Christ Jesus** (see "Word Study"). Only his closest associates were called "fellow workers" (NIV). This dedicated couple surely fit into that category. They had helped Paul get started and finish his work in Corinth. They had stayed in Ephesus and become the nucleus of the believers. They had been mentors for Apollos.

Romans 16:4 mentions something else they did. Paul wrote, "They risked their lives for me" (NIV), they "risked their own necks for my life" (HCSB). **Laid down** is *hupethekan.* It means "to put under." *Trachelon* means **necks.** Literally, they "put their necks under" (the ax). Executions were often by beheading with an ax or a sword. Thus in some way Priscilla and Aquila had made themselves vulnerable to death for Paul. If we take this literally, they "risked their lives" for Paul (NIV). The most likely occasion was the riot in Ephesus (Acts 19:23-41). The power of the good news in Ephesians converted many idol worshipers. There was a temple to the goddess Diana. The men who made and sold images of Diana lost money as a result of the power of the gospel. These idol makers blamed Paul for this loss of income. They rioted and wanted to get their hands on Paul. Nothing is said of Aquila and Priscilla in Acts 19, but they may have risked their lives for him at that time. Paul also wrote of fighting with wild beasts at Ephesus (1 Cor. 15:32). And he mentioned having a death sentence passed on him (2 Cor. 1:8-9). These allusions may refer to the riot, or they may refer to some other crisis. Very likely, during one of those crises that threatened Paul's life, Aquila and Priscilla risked death to save Paul's life.

Paul said that his response to their self-sacrifice was to **give thanks.** He gave thanks to God for them, and he thanked them personally. Paul added that their love was known throughout **all the churches of the Gentiles.** They joined with Paul in giving thanks for this remarkable couple.

On September 11, 2001 our nation watched in horror at the terrible events that took place. Many people died. Among the dead were those who risked and gave their lives trying to help others. Police officers and fire fighters were among that number, as well as some ordinary citizens. The military speaks of their role as putting themselves in harm's way. They place themselves between those they protect and those who threaten them.

Throughout history and in the world today are many Christians who risked and gave their lives for the cause of Christ. Lottie Moon, the missionary to China for whom the Southern Baptist Christmas Offering for International Missions is named, said, "I would that I had a thousand lives that I might give them for the women of China."

What are the lasting lessons in Romans 16:3-4?

1. Christian families work together with others to do God's work.
2. Christians should be willing to give their lives for others.
3. Christians should express thanks to and for other believers.

Open Our Homes for Christian Fellowship (Rom. 16:5a; 1 Cor. 16:19)

How were Aquila and Priscilla able to move about so much? Why did they move so often? What are house churches? What does it take to open your house for church meetings?

Romans 16:5a: **Likewise greet the church that is in their house.**

1 Corinthians 16:19: **The churches of Asia salute you. Aquila and Priscilla salute you much in the Lord, with the church that is in their house.**

Paul wrote 1 Corinthians when he was in Ephesus (1 Cor. 16:8). This was after he returned and launched his long ministry there. Paul's ministry in Ephesus had been highly successful. During that time, the word of God became known throughout the Roman province of Asia (Acts 19:8-10). Thus he sent greetings from **the churches of Asia.** Revelation 2–3 contains letters from the living Lord to seven of the churches of Asia.

Aquila and Priscilla were still living in Ephesus at the time Paul wrote 1 Corinthians. Because they were known in the Corinthian church, Paul sent greetings from them and from **the church that is in their house.** Later, Aquila and Priscilla went to Rome. Paul wrote the church to greet not only Aquila and Priscilla but also **the church that is in their house.**

These verses bring forward two issues: (1) the mobility of Aquila and Priscilla, and (2) the house churches. This couple was first at Rome; then they moved to Corinth. From there they went to Ephesus, and then they came back to Rome. In our day of rapid transportation, we wonder how a couple could have been so mobile in the first century. The Roman Empire had a good system of roads. The government enforced law and order along the roads and sea routes. There were no national boundaries. Thus the couple may have moved often and far, but that was typical of their day. We know why they made some of these moves. They moved from Rome because of Claudius's edict expelling the Jews. They moved to Ephesus from Corinth to provide a nucleus of a church there. They may have moved from Ephesus because of the riot. We don't know all the reasons for their moves, but we do know that wherever they were they were faithful servants of the Lord.

In at least two of the cities, Aquila and Priscilla opened their houses as meeting places for the church. Christians did not build special buildings for churches until the third century. Prior to that time they usually met in someone's house (Acts 12:12; 18:7; Col. 4:15; Philem. 2). In Ephesus Paul used a rented hall as a base (Acts 19:8-9). One reason for house churches was the ever-present danger of persecution. Large groups made them more vulnerable. Opening one's house for church meetings was dangerous. The family had to make sacrifices to make their house available on a regular basis. Another factor was the value of small groups for learning and fellowship.

House churches are found today, especially in lands where Christians are persecuted. China has many such churches. Some churches in free lands combine house meetings with a large meeting of people from all the houses. Most churches meet by classes or by other groups in private homes. Most often this is for fellowship, but sometimes for instruction or evangelism.

If you moved to a place with no churches, would you invite people into your house for prayer and Bible study? Would you seek to plant a new church? This couple did.

What are the lasting lessons in Romans 16:5a and 1 Corinthians 16:19?

1. Christians should have a mobile faith that they practice wherever they go.

2. Christian couples should open their homes for church meetings.

❖ *Spiritual Transformations*

Aquila and Priscilla were a married couple who worked with Paul, Apollos, and others to do the work of God. When Paul came to Corinth, Aquila and Priscilla provided him a place to stay, a way to support himself, Christian fellowship, and a base of operations. When they recognized something lacking in Apollos, they invited him into their home and taught him the way of God more accurately. Paul thanked them for risking their own lives to save his. In both Ephesus and Rome, they had a church meeting in their house.

Aquila and Priscilla are Bible examples of what Christian families ought to be and to do. We should be working together with the church to do the work of God. We can help younger believers fulfill their potential. We can practice in our families and in our lives the self-sacrificial love we know in Christ. We can open our homes for church meetings and fellowship with other believers.

*What should your family be doing to further God's work?*________

____

*What is your family doing to further God's work?*______________

____

Prayer of Commitment: Lord, help me and my family do our part in Your work. Amen.